GERMAN SOCIAL DEMOCRACY

BERTRAND RUSSELL

SPOKESMAN

First published in 1896
This edition published in 2000 by
Spokesman
Russell House
Bulwell Lane
Nottingham
NG6 0BT
Phone 0115 9708318. Fax 0115 9420433.
e-mail elfeuro@compuserve.com
www.spokesmanbooks.com

ISBN 0 85124 571 4

A CIP Catalogue record is available from the British Library.

Printed by Russell Press Ltd (phone 0115 9784505)

Preface to the new edition

Bertrand Russell's first book, on *German Social Democracy*, last appeared in 1965. Then he explained that he had made no effort to revise the book, having "left it as a historical document in which a former writer comments on a former world". He was overly modest about being a "former writer", and in fact after 1965 he published half a dozen works, including one undisputed masterpiece, his three volume *Autobiography*.

But the world of his six lectures had assuredly changed beyond recognition. To begin with, the London School of Economics itself is not at all what it was. Russell was its first lecturer, recruited by the Webbs. The School was yet to evolve into its awesome institutional shape, which was at one time and then another to generate rigorously conservative economic doctrines on the one side, and intermittent student rebellions on the other. But we are here concerned with earlier days: there seems to have been no turbulence during Russell's lectures, while he informed the young people about the theoretical foundations of Marxism, and the idiosyncrasies of Lassalle.

The Marx who was presented in these lectures owes a great deal to the orthodoxy of his German followers. Surprisingly little of Marx's own writing was available in 1895, when Russell was making his enquiries in Germany, still less in London the following year when these lectures were delivered. So Russell may be excused for believing that the iron law of wages was a Marxian doctrine: but this belief remained with him for most of his life. Such is the persistence of what is learned in youth.

What Russell did get right was Marx's argument about the concentration of capital. But the exposition of the doctrines of the Social Democrats is neither the most interesting part of this book, nor the most accurate. Of course, Russell changed his own opinions. He had been a Liberal, not only during his stay in Germany, but long after his lectures and the publication of this book. He did not join the Labour Party until 1914. After he had become a socialist, he was to move far to the left of the German Social Democrats whose late nineteenth century views he had analysed here in his debut as a writer. The extent of this movement can easily be seen in the little book *Roads to Freedom*, which was to be published in 1918, shortly before he was imprisoned for his opposition to the war which brought Britain and Germany into murderous conflict. Both books reflect Russell's suspicion of the state: but in every other respect, they are sharply different.

But if Russell's own opinions changed so markedly, his book retains an appeal. Strangely, it is in Russell's Liberal prejudices that we can see affinities with two quite different traditions: on the one hand the sociological elitism of Roberto Michels' classic study, and on the other with the practical elitism of Leninist principles of party organisation. Russell tells us that the democracy of the Social Democrats' Erfurt programme enunciates the principle that "the ignorant voter is as good a judge of current questions as the member who has specially studied them". This echoes his own famous joke to the Webbs, to the effect that the leaders of a democracy cannot possibly be more stupid than its members, since however stupid such leaders may actually be, the electors are even more stupid to have elected them. Beatrice Webb, he later told us, was not amused by this insight.

The Erfurt doctrine, he says, would "undoubtedly make all wise and expert government impossible". That is why representative government is necessary, because it alone affords any possibility of mobilising special skill and knowledge. Later, Roberto Michels produced, in 1915, his book *Political Parties: A Sociological Study of the Oligarchical Tendencies of Modern Democracy.* This was based upon a close study of German social democracy, with counter-pointing arguments from experience in Socialist Parties in Italy and France. Michels, too, felt that the mass of Party membership was not competent either to decide or to enforce policy decisions, so that there arose an "iron law of oligarchy", in which decision-making became the prerogative of a ruling group, conferring power which would not willingly be foregone: so, "socialists may rule, but socialism, never".

The paradoxical response to this perception was that of Lenin, who developed the argument for a leadership party of professional revolutionaries, whose ethos would counter all popular lethargy and sloth, until every cook had learned to govern.

Traversing this territory, we can see how very true it is that in these pages Russell describes a former world. But it is unfortunately a world that is not without interest, from which lessons may still be drawn, long after the fall of the Kaiser and the confiscation of his Empire.

Ken Coates
June, 2000

Preface to the first edition

The following six Lectures were delivered at the London School of Economics and Political Science in February and March 1896. They are not intended to supply a full history of Social Democracy in Germany, but rather to bring into relief those aspects of such a history which seemed to the author to have been the most important in producing the present political situation. The principle of selection, accordingly, has been throughout to emphasise the events and the speculations which have led to the actual state of feeling. Thus in treating of Marx, I have confined myself to those parts of his work which have chiefly influenced Socialistic opinion in Germany, and have treated very slightly the second and third volumes of *Das Kapital*, which have not yet, so far as I was able to discover, had any considerable influence in modifying the effects of the first volume.

Again, in the Lecture on Lassalle, I have laid far more stress on his debts to Marx than on those to Rodbertus; not because the latter were less important in Lassalle himself, but because, so far as his political effect is concerned, the views he owed to Rodbertus had little result; while those which came from Marx, on the contrary, bore good fruit, both directly and indirectly, in the subsequent growth of Social Democracy.

My acknowledgements are due to my wife for constant help, both by criticism and by collection of material; also to all the German Socialists, whether leaders or followers, with whom I have come in contact, for their uniform courtesy, and for their kind assistance in supplying information.

A bibliography of the principal works consulted is appended.

Bertrand Russell

CONTENTS

LECTURE I

MARX AND THE THEORETICAL BASIS OF SOCIAL DEMOCRACY

" WE German Socialists," says Engels, " are proud of our descent, not only from Saint-Simon, Fourier, and Owen, but also from Kant, Fichte, and Hegel. The German labour-movement is the heir of German classical philosophy."

This haughty claim expresses the peculiar feature which gives to Social Democracy an interest and a human value beyond that of any ordinary political movement. For Social Democracy is not a mere political party, nor even a mere economic theory; it is a complete self-contained philosophy of the world and of human development; it is, in a word, a religion and an ethic. To judge the work of Marx, or the aims and beliefs of his followers, from a narrow economic standpoint, is to overlook the whole body and spirit of their greatness. I shall endeavour, since this aspect of the movement is easily lost sight of in the details of history, to bring it into prominence by a brief preliminary account of Marx's philosophy, showing the sources from which it sprang, and the motives which led him to give it an economic form.

Marx was born in 1818, and grew up at the time when the influence of Hegel's philosophy in Germany was at its height. In every university it was taught and believed; its jargon was familiar to all, and its spirit, in one form or another, animated every intelligent student. But Hegel's spirit was sufficiently broad to contain, among its disciples, the most various and even contradictory tendencies. He was great, on the one hand by his metaphysical results, on the other by his logical method; on the one hand as the crown of dogmatic philosophy, on the other as the founder of the dialectic, with its then revolutionary doctrine of historical development. Both these aspects of Hegel's work revolutionised thought, but in their practical bearing they diverged widely. While the practical tendency of his *metaphysic* was, and is, to glorify existing institutions, to see in Church and State the objective embodiment of the Absolute Idea, his *dialectic method* tended to exhibit no proposition as unqualified truth, no state of things as final perfection. It is not necessary to explain, in a lecture on Marx, the logical function of the dialectic; but the historical application, which reappears in his book " Capital," must be briefly indicated. Since, to Hegel, the reality of the world is only thought, the logical development of thought, from the simplest to the most complex forms, must reproduce itself in the historical development of things. The validity of this view we need not here examine; it is sufficient to point out that

Hegel, in his "Philosophy of History," endeavoured to exhibit the actual course of the world as following the same necessary chain of development which, as it exists in thought, forms the subject of his logic. In this development, everything implies, and even tends to become, its opposite, as son implies father; the development of the world therefore proceeds by action and reaction, or, in technical language, by thesis and antithesis, and these become reconciled in a higher unity, the synthesis of both. Of this process we have an example in Marx's doctrine of the development of production: First, he says, in the savage and the patriarchal eras, we have production for self; a man's goods and the produce of a man's labour are intended solely for his own consumption. Then, in the capitalistic era, the age of exchange and commerce, people produce exclusively for others; things become commodities, having exchange-value, and destined to be used by others than the producers. This is, in technical language, the negation or antithesis of production for self; the two find their synthesis in the communistic state, in production by society for itself. Here the individual still produces for others, but the community produces explicitly—as in the capitalistic era it produces implicitly—for itself. The communistic state ought, according to the development-conception of the dialectic method, to form the starting-point of a new triad, the thesis for a new antithesis; but if this idea ever occurred to Marx, he must have thought that "sufficient unto the day is the evil thereof," for he nowhere gives a hint of anything better than the socialistic community.

This, then, Marx accepted from Hegel : that the development of the world runs parallel with the development of thought, and that both proceed by the dialectic method. But here ends his debt to Hegel. It is often supposed, especially by opponents of Socialism, that his debt was much larger ; that he accepted the glorification of the State to which Hegel's philosophy was supposed to lead ; but this, though partially true of Lassalle, is, as applied to Marx, a " ridiculous fallacy," as Mr. Bosanquet says,[1] and one which it is important to avoid. Through the influence of Feuerbach, and by contact with the French philosophers of his day, Marx early became a thorough-going materialist, and thus abandoned entirely what he calls " the mystifying side of the Hegelian dialectic." To Marx, the movement of history runs parallel to that of thought, not because, as with Hegel, the world is thought, but because thought is the mere outcome and product of material things, which govern all its motions. " My dialectic," says Marx, " is not only different from Hegel's, but is its direct opposite. To Hegel, the life process of the human brain is the demiurgos of the real world, and the real world is only the external, phenomenal form of ' the Idea.' With me, on the contrary, the ideal is nothing else than the material world reflected by the human mind,

---

[1] Editor's Preface to Dr. Schäffle's "Impossibility of Social Democracy," London, 1892, p. vii. How much more Marx was influenced by Hegel's method than by his results, is well illustrated in the sentence : "or, la métaphysique, la philosophie toute entière se résume, d'après Hegel, dans la méthode."—*Misère de la Philosophie*, 1847, p. 93.

and translated into forms of thought. . . . In its mystified form, dialectic became the fashion in Germany, because it seemed to transfigure and to glorify the existing state of things. In its rational form it is a scandal and an abomination to bourgeoisdom and its doctrinaire professors, because it includes in its comprehension and affirmative recognition of the existing state of things, at the same time also, the recognition of the negation of that state, of its inevitable breaking up; because it regards every historically-developed social form as in fluid movement, and therefore takes into account its transient nature not less than its momentary existence; because it lets nothing impose upon it, and is in its essence critical and revolutionary." [1]

Thus Marx is at once logically a dialectical rationalist and metaphysically a dogmatic materialist. These two qualities together account for the main characteristics of that " materialistic theory of history " which forms the basis of Social Democratic politics. From his interpretation of the dialectic, two remarkable features of that theory flow: the revolutionary character, and the inevitableness, almost fatality, of all development. The revolutionary character arises from the logical, as opposed to biological or psychological, nature of the dialectic process: between one conception and its opposite, as between father and son, no gradual transition, no imperceptible organic growth, is possible: logical ideas are clear-cut, sharply defined one against another, and incapable of a Darwinian evolution. Hence the philosophy of history which sees, in successive states of society,

[1] Preface to second edition of " Capital."

successive embodiments of logically distinct ideas, is forced to regard all progress, all development, as proceeding by sudden strides, by revolutions, not necessarily in the sense which the police attach to the word, but in the sense of discontinuous changes from one form of society to a totally different form. Thus, the capitalistic form, in Marx's doctrine, is to continue, despite the growing opposition of the proletariat, until suddenly the "integument is burst asunder, the knell of capitalist private property sounds. The expropriators are expropriated." [1]

Marx's doctrine is thus in a theoretical sense revolutionary, to a degree never attained by any former theory of the world. But practically, the revolutionary tendency is neutralised and held in check by the other quality of development, also due to the dialectic method, the quality of inherent necessity and fatality. All change is due to an immanent principle in the actual order of things; in Hegelian phrase this order contains contradictions, which lead to its final ruin by a new order, in turn to suffér a similar disruption and euthanasia. Nothing, therefore, can hinder the predetermined march of events; the present logically involves the future, and produces it from its own inherent unrest. This fatalism, more than all else, gives to Social Democracy its religious faith and power; this inspires patience, and controls the natural inclination to forcible revolution. There is an almost oriental tinge in the belief, shared by all orthodox Marxians,

---

[1] "Capital," vol. i. p. 789. The references, for the first volume of "Capital," are to the English translation, fourth edition, 1891; for the other volumes, to the German edition of 1894.

that capitalistic society is doomed, and the advent of the communist state a foreordained necessity. As a fighting force, as an appeal to men's whole emotional nature, Social Democracy gains inestimable strength from this belief, which keeps it sober and wise through all difficulties, and inspires its workers with unshakable confidence in the ultimate victory of their cause.

But these characteristics are shared, to some extent, by all new religions; it is Marx's materialism which gives to the movement which he founded its peculiar form and programme. Since mind has been produced by matter, its ultimate motives for action are to be found in material things; the production of these is, accordingly, the moving force which underlies all human phenomena. This transition is nowhere clearly set forth, and is obviously incapable of logical proof; but the outcome of it is this, that all human institutions and beliefs are ultimately, in the last analysis, the outcome of economic conditions, of the conditions, that is, of production and exchange of material things. Not that every motive is economic, *i.e.*, desire for wealth, but that economic motives, where whole societies are concerned, are the prime movers, the stick, to use a vulgar metaphor, which beat the dog and so got the pig over the stile. Religion, science, the State—in short, all branches of human activity—are, in the last resort, determined by economic causes. This is the great leading idea of Marx's view of history; this it is which makes a religion and a philosophy, coextensive with human life, assume the specially economic form of a work on Capital.

This materialistic theory of history, which under-

lies his whole work, is thus expressed by his friend
Engels :—

> " In every historical epoch, the prevailing mode of
> economic production and exchange, and the social organisa-
> tion necessarily following from it, form the basis upon which
> is built up, and upon which alone can be explained, the
> political and intellectual history of that epoch ; conse-
> quently the whole history of mankind (since the dissolution
> of primitive tribal society, holding land in common owner-
> ship) has been a history of class-struggles, contests between
> exploiting and exploited, ruling and oppressed classes." [1]

It must be said, in fairness to Marx, that he did
not rely on the above *à priori* argument for proof of
the correctness of his view.   On the contrary, he
and Engels undertook considerable historical investi-
gations, almost entirely confined to England, in which
they sought to exhibit the economic causes under-
lying all the great changes in human institutions
and beliefs.   Marx learnt, from the disciples of
Ricardo, to regard economic gain as the sole motive
of economic action ; he learnt from contemporary
French Socialists and English life, to regard economic
action as coextensive with human activity.   Thus
as, in economic theory, he accepted in their crudest
form the tenets of orthodox English economists, so,
in his view of human nature, he generalised their
economic motive so as to cover all departments of
social life.   Hence, although he is a reaction against
" bourgeois economics," as he calls it, he retains—as
reactions usually do—much of what he combats, far
more, indeed. than is retained by most modern

[1] Preface to the authorised translation of the Manifesto of the
Communist Party, p. 5.   London, William Reeves, 1888.

economists. In his facts, his authorities, his economic theory, he appeals almost always to the England of his time; the England of 1840–1870 has therefore become, to the Social Democrats, what the land of Canaan was to the Covenanters—the land from which all illustrations are drawn, on which all theories of what is and what ought to be are based. He calls England perpetually "the classic land of capitalism;" the England of to-day, he is convinced, represents the France of to-morrow, and the Germany of the day after. The shrewd Lancashire manufacturer, to him, as to the Manchester school, is the type of all mankind; for Social Democrats, who quote their facts more often from Marx than from life, this overweening influence of English conditions has, I think, been a source of much confusion and false judgment, though also of superiority to the antediluvian paternal views of many German economists and German rulers.

At the University, Marx had studied philosophy with a view to an academic career. His advanced radicalism, however, made this impossible. He therefore become a journalist, and already in 1842, when he was only twenty-four, he obtained the editorship of a Rhenish radical newspaper. This led him to study economics, and one of the first economists whom he read was Proudhon, who was something of a philosopher as well, and endeavoured to popularise Hegel for French consumption. From Proudhon Marx was led to Proudhon's socialist predecessors. After his journal had been suppressed by the police for its advanced views, he went to Paris, and became a follower of the French

Socialists.   Here he made the acquaintance of
Engels, who remained his most intimate friend
through life, and helped him, to an extent which
cannot now be estimated, in all his later work.
Engels was the son of a German manufacturer, but
had lived in Manchester to manage a branch of his
father's business, and had been led to socialism by
the study of English conditions.   Marx soon out-
grew the influence of Proudhon, and in a polemical
work, "The Poverty of Philosophy" (1847), an
answer to Proudhon's "Philosophy of Poverty," he
advocated the superiority of the English socialists,
Bray, Thompson, &c., with whom he had probably
been made acquainted by Engels.

But the first great work in which Marx and
Engels gave expression to their philosophy of life
was the Communist Manifesto, produced at the
request of an International Communist Congress
held in London in 1847.   This work, which is
almost unsurpassed in literary merit, gives the main
points, with the exception of the theory of surplus
value, in Marx's political and historical creed, without the tedious economico-Hegelian pedantry of
"das Kapital."   For terse eloquence, for biting wit,
and for historical insight, it is, to my mind, one of
the best pieces of political literature ever produced.
"A spectre is stalking through Europe," it begins,
"the spectre of Communism.   All the powers of
ancient Europe have combined against this spectre
in a holy war of persecution—the Pope and the
Czar, Metternich and Guizot, French radicals and
German police."   What Communism is, the manifesto then tells in condensed, powerful words.   The

history of all previous society is the history of class struggles; but our epoch has simplified class-oppositions. More and more, society is divided into two great hostile camps, bourgeoisie and proletariat. The modern state is only a committee of the bourgeois class, though historically the bourgeoisie has played a highly revolutionary rôle. Wherever it has come into power, it has destroyed all feudal, patriarchal, idyllic relations, and left no nexus between man and man but that of cash payment. It has, in a word, substituted, for exploitation concealed in religious and political illusions, open, shameless, direct, brutal exploitation. It has transformed the doctor, the lawyer, the parson, the poet, and the man of science into its paid wage-earners. It has torn from the family its touching sentimental veil, and reduced it to a purely monetary relation.

But the bourgeoisie cannot exist without perpetually revolutionising the instruments and conditions of production, and with them all social relations. All firm relations grown rusty, with their train of venerable ideas and opinions, are dissolved, all new ones grow antiquated before they can ossify. Everything established and permanent vanishes into smoke, everything holy is desecrated, and people are forced at last to see their reciprocal relations with sober eyes. By its rapid improvement of the means of production and communication, the bourgeoisie drags all countries, even the most barbarous, into civilisation. It masses the population in huge towns, centralises property in a few hands, and hence produces political centralisation. In a bare century of domination, the bourgeoisie has brought forth more massive and colossal productive forces than all past generations put together. The economic means on which it raised itself were produced by feudalism, but the growth of productive forces at last made feudalism a fetter; this fetter had to be broken; it was broken. In its place came free competition, with the corresponding social and political constitution, with the economic and political rule of the bourgeoisie.

Under our eyes a similar movement is taking place. Modern bourgeois society is like the necromancer who can no longer control the subterranean forces which he has conjured forth. The history of industry and commerce in the last decades is only the history of the revolt of the modern forces of production against the form of property which is the necessary condition of bourgeois existence. Periodic crises, due to over-production, mark the insufficiency of the economic form to the productive powers of society. The weapons with which the bourgeoisie destroyed feudalism now direct themselves against the bourgeoisie itself.

But not only has it forged the weapons which are bringing its death; it has created also the men who are to bear those weapons—the modern workmen, the proletariat. In the same measure in which the bourgeoisie develops, the proletariat also develops—the class which lives only so long as it finds work, and finds work only so long as it increases capital. The labourer, who must sell himself piecemeal, is a commodity like any other—his price, like that of all commodities, is the cost of his production, that is, the bare necessaries for existence and reproduction. But by the competition of capitalists, the small men are driven from the field, and sink into the ranks of the proletariat; only the great capitalists survive, and the proletariat is recruited from all classes of society. The development of industry itself brings the workmen into contact with each other, and forms the means for their combination—their early battles serve only as helps to this end of co-operation. Only union is required to transform isolated battles into a universal class war, and every class war is a political war. The conditions of life of established society are already annihilated in the life of the proletarian; his relation to wife and child has nothing in common with the bourgeois relation; law, morals, religion, are for him so many bourgeois prejudices, behind which lurk so many bourgeois interests. All former conquering classes sought to assure the state of life which they had already won, but the proletariat possesses nothing to secure —he has only to destroy all private security. His is an essentially international war, and the party of the proletariat must be an international party. Everywhere, the communists support all revolutionary parties, whose fundamental motive is always the question of property. "Communists disdain to conceal their views and their purposes. They openly declare that their ends can only be attained by the forcible destruction of all existing social order. May the propertied classes tremble before a communist revolution. The proletariat have nothing to lose by it but their chains. They have a world to conquer. Proletariat of all countries, unite!"

In this magnificent work, we have already all the

epic force of the materialistic theory of history:
its cruel, unsentimental fatality, its disdain of morals
and religion, its reduction of all social relations to
the blind action of impersonal productive forces.
Not a word of blame for the cruel revolutions of the
bourgeoisie, not a word of regret for the ironically-
pictured idylls of the mediæval world.   There is no
question, in Marx, of justice or virtue, no appeal to
human sympathy or morality; might alone is right,
and communism is justified by its inevitable victory.
Marx believes, it is true, that capitalism produces
misery, while communism will produce happiness;
he hates capital with a hatred which often vitiates
his logic; but he rests his doctrine, not on the
"justice" preached by Utopia-mongers (as he calls
his socialist predecessors), not on sentimental love
of man, which he never mentions without immeasur-
able scorn, but on historical necessity alone, on the
blind growth of productive forces, which must, in
the end, swallow up the capitalist who has been
compelled to produce them.   In his "Capital" we
have a carefully attempted proof, illustrated by
immense experience and reading, of these laws of
historical development; in the Communist Manifesto,
a proof could not be attempted, but the essential
points of the doctrine are stated with a force and
eloquence which his later work nowhere attains.
His "Capital" completes the economic theory by the
doctrine of surplus value, and drops the crudely
revolutionary standpoint of the Manifesto.   But the
theory of surplus value, besides being false, is unnecessary, nay even antagonistic, to his theory of
the concentration of capital, and therefore adds

little to the value of his work. We must now, however, leave the imaginative and poetical aspect of
Marx's system, and examine the dry and tedious
details of his economic theory. It will be seen, as
we proceed, that much of this theory is false, and
that its falseness destroys the certainty of that
historical development on which he relied for the
advent of Communism.

In his "Critique of Political Economy" (1859),
and more fully in his "Capital" (1867), his theory
is developed with much logical subtlety, immense
knowledge, and a patience often exceeding that of
the reader. It has two cardinal points: the doctrine
of *Mehrwerth*, or Surplus-Value, and the doctrine of
the concentration of Capital. These two do not
stand or fall together; indeed the former seems to
spring rather from his desire to prove the wickedness of capital than from logical necessity, for it
shows, if anything, that every capitalist must grow
rich, and so destroys that intense competition on
which the concentration of capital must depend.
Both doctrines are implicitly believed by almost all
Social Democrats, and have therefore a practical, as
well as a theoretical, importance. We will begin
with

Marx's Theory of Value.[1]

Ricardo had said: The value of a commodity is
measured by the quantity of labour involved in its

---

[1] In what follows, the text refers exclusively to the first volume
of the "Capital." The two later volumes add little to Marx's
system, and, owing to their late publication (vol. ii. 1885, vol. iii.

production. To this he had added certain qualifications, especially as to capital. These were, however, omitted by Marx. Marx's proof that labour is the only source of value does not resemble Ricardo's, but bears traces of the philosophy of his youth. He says: Exchange-value cannot be a property peculiar to the thing possessing it, but must be one which it shares in common with all the things for which it will exchange; otherwise the equation of values would be unmeaning. Now the only common property of all commodities is that they are produced by human labour, not by this or that human labour, but by "undifferentiated human labour;" this then, he says, must be the essence of value. Quantity of value must be measured by quantity of labour, *i.e.*, by labour-time. Differences in the remuneration of labour only arise from differences in the labour required for its production.[1] The cost of labour-power, then, as of every other commodity, is solely measured by the labour required for its production, *i.e.*, for the production of the labourer's necessaries of life. Wages, therefore, are equal to the value of the necessaries of the labourer, or rather, since the race has to be continued, of the labourer and his family.

But the labourer, in a day, is able to produce more than his necessaries. Suppose that in six

1894), they have little historical importance for the development of Social Democracy. Moreover, the third volume is so inconsistent with the first, that it is difficult to make statements which are true of both. A few of these inconsistencies will be pointed out in footnotes.

[1] In one place, however, in a note, Marx admits a monopoly value of the labour of unusually strong men. Footnote, p. 179.

hours the labourer can replace his necessaries, while his working-day is twelve hours; then the value of his produce, being measured by twelve hours, is double the value of his wages, these being only measured by six hours. The capitalist, therefore, obtains, as *surplus-value*, the whole produce of the last six hours' work, which constitutes his profit. Hence, by purchasing labour-power at the ordinary market rate, the capitalist is able to exploit the labourer, and grow rich by keeping the labourer at the starvation level. This is the necessary result of capitalistic production under a system of free competition; only production by society for society can stop this system of exploitation.

I have endeavoured to put the above argument in as convincing a form as possible, but I fear it will hardly have sounded very cogent. Indeed, it has been rejected by all orthodox economists, and every step, down to the establishment of surplus-value, contains at least one fallacy.

In the first place, the value of a commodity is not measured by the quantity of labour involved. Marx's proof is fallacious in *method;* we can never be sure, by mere abstraction of differences, that we have hit on the *only* common quality of a number of things, or that the quality we have hit on is the relevant one. His proof is fallacious in *substance*, for commodities have also another common quality, utility namely, or the power of satisfying some need. His proof is further invalidated by the omission of the necessary reservations as to capital, and would be false even if cost of production alone measured value. Ricardo's proof that value is measured by labour is somewhat obscure, and will not, I fear, bear the form which I am about to give it, but this is the only form in which it can be said to be logically valid. The proof, then, should be as follows: In a state of free competition, the exchange-value of an article whose production can be indefinitely increased will, in the long run and apart from fluctuations, be measured by its cost of production; its cost of production must—since capital is only accumulated labour—consist, abstracting from interest on capital, of wages alone; now wages are proportional to labour-time, therefore exchange-value is measured by labour-time. In this form, the proposition would, in the main and apart from important qualifications, be substantially true, at least of commodities whose production does not yield a rent. But Marx keeps the conclusion, exchange-value is proportional to labour-time, without an essential step in the argument, namely, wages are proportional to labour-time. He says, on the contrary, wages are equal to the cost of the labourer's necessaries, and are thus independent of the length of his working day. Whether this be true or not, is here irrelevant; what is relevant is, that if this proposition be true, the proposition that value is measured by labour-time must be false. For what is to hinder competition from lowering the price to the point where a business is only just profitable? Again, it is a very vicious use of abstraction to conclude that, even if labour alone determines value, it must be " undifferentiated human labour," that is, labour apart from all qualitative differences, which determines value. Differences in the remuneration of labour are not wholly due to differences in its cost of production; a successful Queen's Counsel costs no more to produce than any briefless barrister. Skill has a value independent of its cost; it commands, as a matter of fact, a mono-poly-rent in the market, and this rent appears in the value of the product.

Again, in all branches of production which yield a rent, it is not the *average* cost of production, but the *greatest* cost of production—*i.e.*, the cost on the margin of cultivation—which determines value. It is the omission of this limitation which makes rent unintelligible to Marx, and leads him to regard it as derivative from profits.[1]

To recapitulate: Ricardo proved that, in a state of free competition, the value of commodities, whose quantity can be indefinitely increased, without increasing the cost of production, is measured by the cost of production; for this is the highest value at which the seller is sure of not being undersold. But Marx says: not cost of production, but labour-time, measures value. By some impalpable meta-physical compulsion, the capitalist must sell the

---

[1] In the third volume, where Marx comes to consider rent, this omission leads him to the grossest inconsistencies. At first he regards rent as the difference between the actual produce and the *average* produce at the same cost (vol. iii., Part ii. pp. 180, 181), without perceiving that this would make the rent negative just as often as positive, since the average, by definition, lies half-way between the best and the worst. On this view, therefore, just as much money would be paid by landlords to farmers, as by farmers to landlords. But a few pages later (p. 192), where he has forgotten the requirements of his theory of value, he gives the ordinary Ricardian theory. Throughout the first volume, he considers only the production, not the distribution, of surplus value, and refuses to regard rent as an independent category.

product of twelve hours' normal labour for a value represented by twelve, though the cost of production is only represented by six. Why, under these circumstances, the capitalist is not forced by competition to reduce his price, Marx does not attempt to explain. Ricardo had sometimes spoken of value as measured by labour-time, because he assumed that, apart from interest, cost of production consisted of wages, and wages were paid by the time. But Marx regards wages as purchase of labour-power, not of labour-time, and thus no reason remains why value should be measured by labour-time.[1]

I have not urged the fundamental objection, which I might have derived from Jevons's theory of value, for the inherent inconsistencies of Marx's view suffice to destroy it, without calling in external aid. But it must be observed, in passing, that Marx usually assumes demand to be a fixed datum, and overcomes the resulting difficulties by a confused and ambiguous notion of "socially necessary labour," which means, at one time, the labour normally necessary for the production of an article, at another, the labour necessary to supply a demand whose amount is supposed constant. The world-wide difference between these two meanings is slurred over, or perhaps quite unperceived, by Marx.

---

[1] In the third volume, Marx admits that commodities may be, and often are, sold below their value in labour-time, without destroying the capitalist's profits. He seems to distinguish between value as the metaphysical embodiment of labour-time, and price, as the amount of other commodities which a given commodity will purchase. He does not perceive, apparently, that if value no longer means *exchange*-value, his whole theory of value falls to the ground. See vol. iii., Part i. pp. 11, 12.

It must also be observed that where cost of production depends on quantity produced—as it must do, wherever Marx's other law, of the concentration of capital, holds good—there cost of production is formally inadequate to determine value. For with different values, there will be different amounts demanded, consequently different amounts produced, and different costs of production. The fluctuation of demand with fluctuating price, or the demand-curve, as it is called, is therefore, in such cases, formally essential for the determination of value.[1]

The total neglect of demand as an economic force is a necessary consequence of the materialistic view of history. For, on this view, material things govern man and all his institutions, and this government is exerted through the agency of blind "productive forces." Production, therefore, is the fundamental fact, and demand is a mere consequence of it. To the modern economist, however, as to the non-materialistic philosopher, demand takes the first place; things are produced only if they may be expected to satisfy some human want; the want makes the utility of the product, and without utility nothing would be produced. A man who produced a new pyramid, or a new Cleopatra's Needle, would not be able to sell them at a price equal to their cost of production. The necessity for taking demand into account, therefore, destroys not only Marx's theory of value, but the whole materialistic theory of history.

But admitting that value is measured by labour-time, what is meant by the labour-time necessary to

[1] Marx admits this later in treating of Rent, vol. iii., Part ii. p. 274.

produce a labourer ?   On the assumption that labour-power is a commodity whose supply can be increased indefinitely—an assumption which is true in the long run, except in periods of rapidly-growing industry, when the demand may grow faster than the supply—" the cost of a labourer," says Marx, is " the socially necessary cost ; " that is, the lowest cost at which he can normally be produced.   This cost consists of the minimum of necessaries required to keep him in health.   But the cost of these necessaries consists in turn of wages ; hence, if there exists, or has existed, a set of labourers whose wages were not at starvation level, the argument breaks down.   Also it is forgotten that labour, unlike other commodities, is not produced by capitalists, but produces itself. Its cost of production, therefore, is determined, wherever wages are above starvation level, by the remuneration at which it thinks it worth while to produce itself, *i.e.*, as Malthusians would say, by the standard of comfort.   It is a question of historical fact, not of logical necessity, whether this standard is, at any time and place, the starvation level or something much higher.   Hence arises the possibility, ignored by Marx, of raising wages by Trade Unions and other methods, which are possible within the " capitalistic state."   It is from overlooking this possibility that the paramount importance, assigned by Marx and his followers to political and State action as opposed to strikes and Unions, has arisen.

There remains one step in the argument by which surplus-value is discovered, and this step, fortunately, is illustrated by examples from the actual accounts of manufacturers.   Suppose the labourer, says Marx, to produce the value of his necessaries in six hours: then this share of the produce alone will fall to wages, and the rest will be pure profit. It is assumed, both in the abstract arguments and, more definitely, in the illustrative examples, that the undertaker does no work and obtains no wages.[1] Whatever, then, in the firm's accounts does not *appear* as wages, is reckoned as unearned profits. Of rent and interest, such a view would be fairly true, but that Marx should have made the monstrous assumption that the undertaker's direction of a business involves no labour, and adds nothing to value, would be incredible if the examples he gives did not clearly prove it.[2]

---

[1] In the third volume, in discussing interest, this assumption is abandoned, and Marx admits both earnings of management and rent of ability, or slyness, as he prefers to call it (vol. iii., Part i. pp. 343, 359, 365). At the same time, for fear the whole discovery of surplus-value should resolve itself into a ponderous theory of interest, he insists that profits contain a portion of pure surplus-value, not resolvable into interest, wages, or rent of ability (pp. 366, 369). Why, in this case, any owner of capital should be willing to content himself with interest rather than profits, since profits are not a compensation for work, Marx does not attempt to explain.

In his theory of interest, also, he is of course unable, consistently with his theory of value, to find any lower limit for interest. Its upper limit, he says, is profits, after earnings of management and rent of ability have been deducted. But this limit, he thinks, it never attains. As for its lower limit, he says, it has none—it *may* sink to any level. Rather, with his value-theory, we should say, it *must* be zero. What really gives the lower limit is the marginal disutility of saving, or rather, the rate at which, in a given state of demand, the supply is just equal to the demand. But this shows interest as the reward of abstinence, and introduces capital, or waiting, as an element in determining value. Rather than make such suicidal admissions, Marx prefers to regard interest as wholly irrational (vol. iii., Part i. pp. 338, 343).

[2] Vol. i. pp. 202, 203.

We have now seen that every step in Marx's argument contains such serious mistakes as alone to vitiate his theory, even if all the other steps were sound. The "great discovery of surplus-value," which most Socialists regard as his claim to immortal renown, cannot, therefore, be held to have any theoretical validity whatever.

At this point it is customary for the self-satisfied German bourgeois to sing a pæan of triumph, and leave Socialism to be devoured by its own inconsistencies. But economic pedantries such as the above do not suffice to answer a whole class of society just awakened to its interests; the unspeakable contempt with which Social Democrats allude to such refuters of Marx, ought to suggest that somehow there must be a kernel of truth in his doctrine after all. And I believe that by a little more pedantry, by the magic words Rent and Monopoly, we can bring out something which, from the standpoint of the working-man, is practically the same as Marx's doctrine—with the one very important exception, however, that such methods as combination among workmen, and factory legislation, without a communistic society, seem able to effect far more of the improvements which Marx desires than he is willing to admit.

The distinction between rent and profits seemed, to the bourgeois economist—if I may adopt for the moment the Marxian way of explaining economic theories—a distinction of great importance, for rent belonged usually to the aristocratic landlord, while profits belonged to the middle-class manufacturer. These formed distinct classes with antagonistic interests, whose conflicts have been most forcibly depicted by Marx himself. To the wage-earner, however, the distinction of rent and profit is irrelevant: wages and not-wages, for him, are the only important divisions of the produce. Marx, therefore, in writing from the labourer's point of view, and with a theory of value on which rent is inexplicable, makes light of this distinction—whatever is not wages is profits, is surplus-value. Now it is self-evident, since some men live in idle luxury, that a labourer normally produces more than he consumes, and that this surplus goes to support idleness. How does this come about? It comes about, in economic language, by monopoly rent; wherever the man or company of large capital is able to produce more easily than the man of small capital, he is able, since large capitals cannot be indefinitely increased at will, to obtain a rent from his advantage, just as the landlord obtains a rent from the superiority of his land to the worst land in cultivation. Wherever, in short, some conditions are more favourable to production than others, while the better conditions cannot be indefinitely increased at will, and production must be carried on also under the worse conditions in order to meet the demand, there those who have a monopoly of the best conditions, obtain a rent from their advantage, and this rent is not the reward of labour, but a surplus-value which the capitalist is enabled to deduct from the labourer's produce. The skilful entrepreneur, in like manner, gets a rent from his monopoly of skill. The skilful artisan, also, gets a monopoly rent, which raises his wages above his cost of production; but the *average* working-man, so long as Marx's reserve-army of labour is kept up, cannot obtain any monopoly-value; the marginal utility of the necessaries of life, to him, is infinite, and therefore outweighs any severity of work; so long, therefore, as the supply of labour is excessive, —and such excess Marx accepts from Malthus, as the law of population proper to a capitalistic society [1] —so long the labourer will be kept at starvation wages, and the excess of his produce over his necessaries will go to the capitalist, whether as rent, profits, or interest. In a state of free competition, it is true, this excess cannot appear as pure profits, for competition will force down the price of commodities to the lowest point at which it is profitable to sell them. But "profitable" here, as in the Ricardian theory of rent, means profitable in the most unfavourable circumstances in which production is permanently carried on;—in other circumstances, there will be a differential rent, appearing as rent or profits according to circumstances.

Where these conditions are satisfied, therefore— where, that is to say, the increase in the supply of labour exceeds the increase in the demand, and where there are no very strong combinations among working-men—there the Iron Law, as applied to unskilled labour, is likely, for the moment, to be true. But so many are the conditions which may overthrow it, and so different is it, when true, from

[1] On the inconsistencies in Marx's theories of population, and on his attitude towards Malthus and the Iron Law, see Julius Wolf, *Sozialismus und kapitalistische Gesellschaftsordnung*, pp. 255-262.

the sense which most Socialists give to it, that it would be better named the Guttapercha Law. When it is true, to begin with, it only means that labourers will be kept at the lowest point at which they think it worth while to work, which lowest point depends on the customary standard of comfort. Again, it could only have any *permanent* truth, even in this modified sense, if the Malthusian principle were correct, that increased comfort leads to larger families. Since the very opposite of this principle seems to be the fact, a sudden or continued increase in the demand for labour, by which wages are raised, for a considerable time, above their former level, so far from being counteracted by the growth of population, may easily be still further augmented by increased prudence among labourers. And even where population is rapidly increasing, the increase of the demand for labour may easily be still more rapid. But besides all these counteracting causes which depend on general economic and social conditions, and are only very partially under the control of the labourers, strong Trade Unions, by supporting the men who are out of work, and so destroying the necessity for concluding a bargain with the employer at any price, may always keep the supply down to the level of the demand, and ensure the highest wages at which the trade can be carried on.

The Marxian theory, therefore, that the price of labour-power is the cost of its production, and that this cost consists of the barest necessaries of life, can only be true under very special circumstances. Nevertheless, the doctrine of surplus value has this kernel of truth, that capitalistic production does enable the recipients of rent and interest to grow rich by idleness, and does, to this extent, mulct labour of a part of the produce. It is also true that, in Germany, where the whole country is poor, and labour is very little organised into Unions, the Iron Law has, for the moment, a certain amount of validity. Marx's doctrines have therefore a sufficient kernel of truth to make them seem self-evident to German workmen. It is unfortunate, however, that their apparent necessity, under a capitalistic régime, should make German labourers very lukewarm as to trade unions, and all non-political means of improving their condition. The exclusively political character of Social Democracy, which is mainly due to Marx, is thus of very doubtful utility. So long as the present persecution lasts, however, it is not likely to undergo any considerable change.

Law of Concentration of Capital.

It remains to consider the tendency to production on a large scale, or law of concentration of capital, which Marx regards as universal, and which forms, I think, the most cardinal point of his whole doctrine. We have already seen, in discussing the Communist Manifesto, how Marx applies this law to prove the necessary advent of Communism, by the ever-increasing power of the unpropertied proletariat, as against the ever-diminishing number of great capitalists. In his " Capital," the same arguments are repeated at greater length. "Accumulation of capital is increase of the proletariat." [1] . . .

---

[1] P. 627.

The first step is the destruction of handicrafts, but when this is complete, the process takes a new form. " That which is now to be expropriated is no longer the labourer working for himself, but the capitalist exploiting many labourers. This expropriation is accomplished by the action of the immanent laws of capitalistic production itself, by the centralisation of capital. One capitalist always kills many. Hand in hand with this centralisation, or this expropriation of many capitalists by few, develop, on an ever extending scale, the co-operative form of the labour process, the conscious technical application of science, the methodical cultivation of the soil, the transformation of the instruments of labour into instruments of labour only usable in common, the economising of all means of production by their use as the means of production of combined socialised labour, the entanglement of all peoples in the net of the world-market, and with this, the international character of the capitalistic régime. Along with the constantly diminishing number of the magnates of capital, who usurp and monopolise all advantages of this process of transformation, grows the mass of misery, oppression, slavery, degradation, exploitation ; but with this too grows the revolt of the working class, a class always increasing in numbers, and disciplined, united, organised by the very mechanism of the process of capitalist production itself. The monopoly of capital becomes a fetter upon the mode of production, which has sprung up and flourished along with, and under it. Centralisation of the means of production, and socialisation of labour, at last reach a point where they become incompatible with their capitalist integument. This integument is burst asunder. The knell of capitalist private property sounds. The expropriators are expropriated." [1]

In Marxian Socialism, the importance of the law of unlimited concentration of capital is supreme. For not only the necessary advent of the collectivist state, but also the great economies which are expected from the public management of production, are wholly dependent on this law. If it be true, as Marx maintains, that in all branches of production the productivity of labour increases with the scale of the business, then it is evident that, if competition be allowed to operate freely, the average size of firms must grow larger and larger, until at last the State will be able to contain only one firm in every kind of business. It is also evident that, since this result is to be attained by the continual cheapening of production, it will, when attained, cause a great increase of the national wealth. This is the reason why Socialists, in picturing the collectivist state, imagine a high degree of comfort to be attainable by very few hours of daily labour. If this law, in its general form, were unexceptionally true, and if, as Marx seems always to suppose,[2] every single business were in the hands of a single capitalist, then, though all the rest of Marx's economic theory should be proved to be false, the sudden revolutionary change from private capital to collective management would seem inevitable. The theory of value and surplus-value, since it can contribute nothing to the proof of this law, is inessential to Socialism as a theory of what will be; the Iron Law of wages

[1] Pp. 788, 789.   [2] But see footnote, p. 35.

is inessential, since, so long as rent and interest exist, the wage-earner has always a motive to urge their appropriation to himself; the doctrine that the labourer's labour-power, not his labour, is bought by the capitalist, is wholly inessential; but the law of concentration of capital is quite essential. If this law were not true, there would, in the first place, be no increase of productivity by collective production; and in the second place, the "proletariat army" whose ever-increasing numbers are finally to overpower the capitalist, would not necessarily acquire supreme power. This has been realised by Conservative politicians and economists in Germany, who are perpetually engaged in schemes for re-establishing the Guilds and "rescuing the handicraftsman:" for the handicraftsman, being the owner of his own capital, usually opposes Social Democracy, as the party of a class to which he feels himself superior. We must therefore examine the law with some care, and endeavour to discover the limits and exceptions to its truth.

Marx, though he treats the law at great length, has nowhere attempted so rigid a proof as could have been desired, and has not preserved a sufficiently sharp distinction between theoretical and statistical proofs. The latter, be it observed, though interesting for their own sake, are here insufficient, for they can never show that we have to do with a tendency to which there are no limits; they can only show that the limits, if they exist, have not yet been reached. It may be, for all that statistics can prove to the contrary, that there is somewhere, in any given state of technique, a point of equilibrium, beyond which new forces come into play, and make a further increase in size unprofitable. This possibility, which is overlooked by Marx, and is not utilised by most of his German critics, forces us to adopt a more theoretical method; we must, by examining particular businesses, discover the general tendencies which make for large or small firms.[1]

In the first place, it is evident that large businesses are more profitable than small ones, wherever there is, on the whole, a law of increasing return, wherever, that is to say, a large output is relatively cheaper to produce than a small one; where, on the contrary, a law of diminishing return prevails, small businesses will be the more profitable. As this fact suggests, the question requires entirely separate treatment for Industry and for Agriculture. We will begin with the former.

In Industry, both productive and distributive, there is, as we can see at once, a very strong tendency to increasing size of firms. The progress of joint-stock companies, the growth of huge shops such as Whiteley's, the decay of handicrafts, all point to the general truth, up to the present time, of Marx's law of the concentration of capital. The first and chief agent in the change has been machinery. Wherever expensive machinery can be used with profit, there the individual handicraftsman, and, with further technical development, the small master, must disappear from the competitive field. A large capital is necessary to set up the

---

[1] The following discussion in the main follows Marshall's "Principles of Economics," 3rd ed., Book iv. chap. xi., and Book vi. chap. x., to which the reader is referred for a fuller treatment.

machinery, and a large number of workmen may
be necessary to work it. Again, the small master
cannot easily get the best machinery ; technical improvements are so rapid that only a large capitalist
with considerable leisure has time enough to find
out what are the best machines, or capital enough
to change them when they become antiquated. A
large firm, also, can experiment more easily in new
methods, and can more easily make known a successful result. The greater facility of advertisement is
an important aid to large firms, as is also the saving
in freight when large quantities of material are to
be transported. Then there is a great advantage in
division of labour, which can only be carried far by
a large firm. Greatest of all, perhaps, is the economy
of skill, though entirely overlooked by Marx, owing
to his glorification of manual labour and contempt
for the head-work of capitalist management. Not
only has the large business a greater choice of suitable foremen, and of workmen suitable for any operation requiring special skill, but the head of a large
firm, also, has more leisure to think out the general
problems of his business and watch the general
movements of the market. Any one who has read
Bagehot's description of the successful city man will
realise the great importance of this leisure ; if a
man at the head of a large firm is busy, says Bagehot, that is a sign that his business is going wrong ;
the successful man should not work more than four
hours a day.[1] This factor, as I remarked before, is
overlooked by Marx ; but it forms, to my mind, a very

---

[1] " Lombard Street," 10th ed., pp. 216, 217 ; and " Physics and
Politics," 1st ed., pp. 189, 190.

fair argument for the management of all technically advanced businesses by a central authority, with no duties but to study the general conditions and the technical possibilities of the business in question.

In distribution, a similar movement has become very marked in recent times; large retail shops save in advertisement, in the possibility of keeping a large stock, and in smaller loss from changes of fashion. In the carrying trade, railways, trams, &c., have so evident an advantage from management on a large scale, that there is no need to point it out.

But in other respects again, there are disadvantages in production on a large scale, and these disadvantages increase with increasing size, so that theoretically, we may suppose, there is a limit, in any given state of technique, to the profitable growth of a business. The chief of these disadvantages is the greater difficulty of superintendence: a large business gives more room for shirking by foremen, for scamping work, and for corruption. Also the advantage derived by the big man from greater trade-knowledge is continually diminishing; with advertisements and trade journals, the best technical knowledge is becoming more and more accessible to all. Again, a very large business must produce, at least in part, for distant places, and has therefore to contend against the expense of transport. This, however, is a rapidly diminishing disadvantage. Then, again, in all branches of production which require artistic taste, and are therefore not reducible to mechanical routine, machinery is inapplicable, and the individual producer must remain supreme. Except for this last, however, which applies only to a very small fraction of production, progress is almost entirely on the side of large firms; superintendence at every point becomes less and less necessary as people grow in intelligence and efficiency, while skill and expensive machinery become every day more and more necessary. On the whole, then, except in artistic production, and in the raising of raw products, which we have still to consider, Marx's law seems true. Although, in any given state of technique, there is a limit, from difficulties of transport and superintendence, to the profitable size of firms, yet this limit, as technique advances, and as competition gives the victory to those who have most power of organisation, continually recedes, and is therefore liable, sooner or later, to become co-extensive with the State. As soon as a business has reached this phase of development, State-management in general becomes profitable, and is likely to be brought about by the combined action of free competition and political forces. In railways, gas and water supply, &c., many Continental governments have already taken this step; the growth of trusts and rings suggests that it might, with profit, be taken in many other businesses.

But three points must be noticed in this process, which make it very different from the process suggested by Marx. First, big firms consist usually of companies, and their victory does not therefore necessarily diminish the number of individual capitalists;[1] secondly, a new middle-class is created

---

[1] In the third volume Marx fully recognises the importance of joint-stock companies, and truly says that they are socialising production within the capitalist state (*e.g.*, vol. iii., Part i. p. 423), but

by large firms and the use of machinery—*e.g.*, foremen, engineers, and skilled mechanics—and this class destroys the increasingly sharp opposition of capitalist and proletariat on which Marx lays so much stress; thirdly, the profitable management of businesses by the State presupposes a certain degree of development, and should therefore be undertaken at different times in different businesses, not, as Marx supposes, by a single revolutionary transformation. This last point is especially important, as it transforms the whole process into one of gradual organic development, instead of the discontinuous dialectical change which Social Democracy expects.

But in agriculture, where the law of diminishing return prevails, the whole development is totally different from that of industry. Marx, as I pointed out in criticising the theory of value, does not adequately distinguish between rent and profits, since both go to the capitalists. He therefore confuses large landlords with large farmers; and adduces, in proof of his contention, many facts which spring from such wholly uneconomic motives as the rich man's desire to "breathe his native air on his own ground," or the love of sport, which led, for example, to the formation of the Scotch deer forests. This is one of the instances on which Marx lays most stress, though it is difficult to see how it forms an argument for farming on a large scale. We must therefore,

he takes no account of the very great *political* difference between this form of the transition to collective production, and the form spoken of in the first volume. That a development governed by the growth of joint-stock companies is likely to be gradual, peaceful, and piecemeal, while the development sketched in vol. i. is revolutionary, does not seem to occur to him.

in discussing agriculture, clearly distinguish the landlord from the capitalist farmer, even where they happen to be the same person. We must also remember—a fact forgotten alike by supporters and opponents of Marx—that the economic size of a farm is not its acreage, but the capital laid out on it. In this sense, many giant farms of Western America may be smaller than a suburban market-garden.

From the law of diminishing return, it follows that, in any given state of demand, more intensive cultivation of a given area cannot be as cheap as less intensive cultivation; there will not, therefore, apart from special conditions of rent or tenure, be any tendency, at a given time, to accumulation of capital in this way. As regards extension of acreage, the same result appears. Increase of acreage— since the labourer, instead of having his work brought to him, as in a factory, has to go to the land — involves a large expenditure of time in moving from place to place, and loses the advantages of concentration, which are so important in large factories and shops. Since the work varies with the seasons, the same machine cannot be continuously employed, and division of labour cannot be carried very far, so that these supreme advantages of large industries are, to a great extent, lost. Again, agricultural skill consists chiefly of special local knowledge of peculiarities of the soil, &c., and in this a small farmer is likely to have an advantage. For these reasons, although every improvement in the use of agricultural machinery favours large farms, there seems good ground for supposing that, at any rate for a long time to come, there will be no considerable tendency to the centralisation of agricultural capital.

Marx's law of the concentration of capital thus breaks down in the raising of raw produce. On this point, all orthodox economists, and even some of the Social Democrats, seem to be agreed. We shall see, later on, what difficulties this confusion of landlord and farmer has brought on Social Democracy, which has never grasped the difference between making the State the landlord and making it the agricultural undertaker. The conditions of German agriculture do not help, as in England, to make this distinction clear; but it is evident that none of the above arguments have any force against the proposal for State ownership of land. For this proposal, as every one knows, the arguments are, if anything, stronger than for any other collectivist measure, yet the peculiar form of Marxian Socialism makes all these arguments logically inaccessible to German Social Democracy.

The law of the concentration of capital is the most original part of Marx's work, and the most essential item in his system. As applied to industry, it is true and important; but with his usual habit of reckless generalisation, he assumed it to be true universally, without sufficiently examining special branches of production. Even in the *ownership* of land, the tendency has been, ever since the break-up of feudalism, in the very opposite direction; in the Irish Land Acts, we have all seen a striking instance in which decentralisation constituted a distinct economic advance.

We have now discussed all the most essential points in Marx's economic doctrines, and have seen that none of them, as a theory of what is, or of what necessarily will be, will stand a thorough criticism. The materialistic theory of history, at any rate in the precise form which it derives from Marx, is not true, and leads to the neglect of demand as an element in determining production and value. The theory that value is determined exclusively by labour-time is false, and is, in particular, inconsistent with the doctrine that the capitalist buys the labourer's labour-power, not his labour-time. The theory that the wage-earner, so long as capitalistic production continues, must be kept at starvation wages, is completely false, as the movements of wages in England and America, or even in Saxony [1]—to say nothing of economic theory—sufficiently prove. Again, the theory that free competition leads necessarily to continually increasing concentration of capital, is wholly false in agriculture, and true only up to a certain limit in industry. That this limit may, however, be often coextensive with the State— *e.g.*, in railways—must be admitted. Finally, the concentration of capital in large firms does not necessarily imply its concentration in a few hands ; the firms may consist—in fact, normally do consist —of many shareholders in a joint-stock company. It may thus easily happen that, in a country where production on a large scale prevails to an immense extent, the number of people interested in the return to capital, and so in the Marxian sense capitalists

[1] For statistics of Saxon incomes, *vide* Julius Wolf, *Sozialismus und kapitalistische Gesellschaftsordnung*, Stuttgart, 1892, pp. 202 ff.

and pillars of bourgeois society—the number of these people, we must maintain, may be very great, and the consequent opposition to capital by no means so overpowering as Marx holds that it must, sooner or later, become. Marxian Socialism, as a body of proved doctrine, must therefore be rejected. But it by no means follows that Collectivism—as a doctrine of what ought to be, or of what, by political and economic development, is likely to be— is at the same time disproved. As a doctrine of necessary fatality, as a body of knowledge which we know to be true, whatever men may do to help or hinder it, Socialism cannot stand criticism any better than the earlier gospel of *Laissez-faire;* a dogmatic denial of the possibility or desirability of a Collectivist State would, however, be equally impossible to substantiate, and the decision must therefore be left to detailed considerations of special circumstances.

Marx is, in a sense, the last of the great German system-makers; it is by his system, in a great measure, that he imposes on the imagination and obtains such ardent disciples, but it is also by his system that he is led into such mistakes as that about agriculture, and that his followers are prevented from advocating any interests but those of the industrial proletariat.

LECTURE II

MARX, whose principal doctrines we have now briefly reviewed, was, as I said in the last lecture, the last of the great German system-makers; in his love of a self-contained system, in his uncompromising generalisations, he was a thorough German, but in the facts and theories on which he relied or against which he argued, he was English through and through. His system is the natural result of the action of English life and English interests on a studious and methodical German mind. But Marx *was* a student, not an agitator; after 1849, when he was only thirty-one, he lived in England, I might almost say in the British Museum, and affected politics chiefly through his influence on a few leading agitators. The growth of this influence, its gradual extension to the mass of the industrial proletariat, and the adoption in Germany, both by rich and poor, of his principle of class-warfare, must form the theme of a history of German Socialism.

The first man who flung Marx's doctrines to the people, who awakened them to a feeling of class-interests, to a revolt against their miserable circumstances, and an ardent political struggle for their rights—the first man, in short, who made the fourth estate a factor in German politics, was Lassalle. Lassalle was, in many respects, the very opposite of Marx. Practical through and through, he could bring all his immense theoretical knowledge to bear on any question of the moment; passionate and powerful, he compelled all with whom he came in contact to follow his leadership; in training and sympathies, a German of the Germans, he was yet, in his character and methods, far more English than Marx. Though he could appreciate, to the full, the desirability of the most radical transformations of society, he realised, also, the necessity of confining himself, in practical agitation, to a single, simple, essential demand. No one has ever understood the power of agitation and organisation better than Lassalle; no one has ever possessed in a greater degree the power of flogging men's minds into enthusiastic activity. The word "agitator," says Brandes, seems to have been created for him. The secret of his influence lay in his overpowering and imperious will, in his impatience of the passive endurance of evil, and in his absolute confidence in his own power. His whole character is that of an epicurean god, unwittingly become man, awakening suddenly to the existence of evil, and finding with amazement that his will is not omnipotent to set it right.

But before we can rightly understand Lassalle's work and aims, we must have some knowledge of the development of Germany up to the time of his appearance in public life.

The Reformation and the Thirty Years' War had destroyed German unity, as it existed under the Holy Roman Empire; the South and much of the

West had remained Roman Catholic, while the North and East had become Protestant. Prussia, the eastern and least-civilised state, with a largely Sclavonic population and a wholly feudal organisation of society, had become, under Frederick the Great, the most powerful of the German monarchies. While the West had been rapidly advancing in culture by contact with France, the East had been drilling its men and perfecting its military organisation, and had acquired a purely military preponderance. In the time of Napoleon, however, the Rhineland was annexed to France, and the feudal power of Prussia was, for the moment, annihilated by the battle of Jena. These two events brought about a great progress in civilisation; the Rhine provinces, the home of Marx, and the chief centre of Lassalle's agitation, learnt the joys of civil freedom, and Prussia learnt the weakness of a purely aristocratic organisation of society. A reliable German authority confesses that the German governments understood the ideas of the enlightenment much better in the school of Napoleon than in that of German philosophers and poets.[1] The serfs were liberated, many aristocratic and feudal rights were abolished, finance was reformed, and the King of Prussia promised a constitution if the people would help to drive out the French from German territory. By these reforms and promises, the people, who had previously been rather friendly than hostile to Napoleon, were roused to national enthusiasm, and fought, in the war of 1813, for political as well as national liberation. But no sooner were the French expelled, than the very

[1] Herkner, *Arbeiterfrage*, p. 66.

patriots to whom Germany owed its independence, when they ventured to remind the king of his promise, were baffled in their hopes of reform, and imprisoned as demagogues.

These repressive measures were successful in all parts of Prussia except the Rhineland; here, where economic development was already tolerably advanced, where French rule had brought civilisation and destroyed feudalism, a democratic movement was kept alive. Here, in 1842, the local democrats founded a paper, in which Karl Marx, then only twenty-four, was first a collaborator, and soon afterwards, in consequence of his brilliant articles, the chief editor. These articles were so skilfully worded that the press censors could find nothing to say against them; they therefore suppressed the paper entirely. Marx, in consequence, went to Paris, where he became acquainted with Engels and with the leading French Socialists. The study of French Socialism led him to accept its doctrines, which he and Rüge advocated in polemical form in the *Deutsch-Französische Jahrbücher.* The enmity to Prussia, which this journal displayed, caused Guizot's ministry to banish Marx from France. He therefore went to Brussels, where he and Engels, at the invitation of the Communist League in London, composed the Communist Manifesto. This appeared in January 1848, a month before the Revolution broke out in France. It is noticeable that neither of its authors knew much of Germany; Marx knew France and the Rhineland, Engels had lived almost entirely in England. While this exile gave them an almost prophetic insight into the course of

German economic development, it destroyed their political insight into the needs of the moment, and is responsible, even now, for much of the unpractical, theoretical attitude of Social Democracy.

The French Revolution of February was succeeded by the German Revolution of March. At first, middle-class and proletariat, town and country, were united; the movement was irresistible, the Prussian king was terrified, and a Constitutive Assembly, without whose consent the king promised to make no new laws, was elected by universal suffrage. But when the demands of the peasants, which extended only to relief from feudal burdens, had been hurriedly granted, their interest in the Revolution collapsed, and they ranged themselves on the side of order. As the socialistic demands of the proletariat—which, by the way, were largely reactionary, and aimed partly at the preservation of guilds—became more and more pronounced, the middle-class became alarmed, and rapidly drifted into reaction. The king recovered his presence of mind, and dissolved the over-democratic assembly; a new one, more amenable to the royal will, was elected, but had still too much spirit to be wholly satisfactory. So the king broke his word, dissolved the chamber, and by a *coup d'état* had a new one elected under an anti-democratic suffrage. This new chamber was wholly reactionary, and consented to the constitution under which Prussia still groans. This constitution left the bulk of the power with the king, and the rest in the hands of the richer burghers. The reaction set in simultaneously in the rest of Germany, and the revolution, owing to

the sudden terror of the middle-class before the
awakened proletariat, failed before it had claimed
the most ordinary civil rights.　Marx, who had
returned to edit the *Neue Rheinische Zeitung*, an
ultra-democratic journal, was finally forced to leave
the country; all the popular leaders were imprisoned
or banished, and by 1850 all remnants of the democratic movement had disappeared.　In this year
most of the laws against organisation were passed,
which up to the present time exercise such a
dangerous and harmful effect on workmen's unions
and societies.

But during the fifties, the economic development
of Germany rapidly advanced.　Freedom in the
choice of trades, and free circulation of labour, could
be granted in the early sixties, without serious
opposition from the handicrafts; increase of trade
and industry strengthened the Progressive Party,
the champion of *laissez-faire* individualism, and the
whole economic organisation became rapidly more
and more modern.　Economists adopted from England and France the principles of Ricardo's disciples,
with their social panacea of free competition and
self-help.　Schulze-Delitzsch, a rich philanthropic
economist of this school, founded a large number of
working-men's friendly societies, and urged the utility
of saving and thrift.　He had a considerable following among the higher class of artisans and handicraftsmen, to whom he preached self-help and the
benevolent action of free competition.　But in some
of the more advanced towns, the men soon began to
feel that Schulze-Delitzsch's gospel was not very complete, and that something better must be possible.

Some of the most intelligent were sent, by the Progressives, to the London Industrial Exhibition of
1862, and returned, doubtless to their patron's sur-
prise, full of heretical views which they had learnt
from English and French Socialists. The chief
centre of the new movement was Leipzig, and it was
the Leipzig workmen's association which, in February
1863, asked Lassalle's opinion as to the course they
should pursue in politics. This was his opportunity,
and with his answer, his agitation and German
practical Socialism began.

Lassalle had already, on many important occasions,
given public expression to his views, in a manner
which had attracted the attention alike of police
and people. But his excursions into practical politics, up to this time, had been desultory and dis-
connected ; study, and the complications of his
private life, had occupied the greater part of his
time. He was born in 1825, of well-to-do Jewish
parents, at Breslau, where the Jews, until 1848,
were not even formally emancipated. As a boy, he
filled his journal with aspirations to liberate his
people, and bitter invectives against their servile
endurance. A little later, his revolt against the
indignities which, as a middle-class Jew, he had
suffered at the hands of the more powerful classes,
converted him into a revolutionary democrat. " Had
I been born a prince," he wrote, with self-knowledge
rare in a youth, " I should have been an aristocrat
heart and soul. But as it is, being the son of a
common bourgeois, I shall in my time be a democrat."
His democratic ambitions led him to abandon, at the
age of sixteen, the trade of merchant, for which his

father had destined him, in favour of an academic training for the career of a popular leader. At the university he worked with immense zeal at philology and philosophy, and, attracted by the very difficulties of the task, he planned a work, not completed, however, until 1857, on Heraclitus, the Obscure Philosopher. A visit to Paris in 1844 gave him an opportunity to study French Socialism, and in the Revolution of '48 he became acquainted with Marx and wrote for the *Neue Rheinische Zeitung.* Having urged the people to armed resistance against the Prussian *coup d'état,,* he was brought to trial in Düsseldorf in May 1849. The speech which he prepared for his defence (*Assisenrede*) was a masterpiece of logical rhetoric, and much has been written, by Brandes and others, of its tremendous effect on the Court. Unfortunately, however, it was never delivered. What really happened, as reported by the *Neue Rheinische Zeitung* of the day, was in the highest degree characteristic.

Lassalle had given the notes of his speech to a printer, and some copies had accidentally got into the hands of the judges. On the ground that the speech was dangerous to order, the President resolved to exclude the public, even the witnesses. Hereupon the following altercation arose[1]:—

"*President.* I call on the defence or the accused to speak.

"*Lassalle.* I have first to make a proposal to the Court. The Court has excluded the public on the ground that my

---

[1] I have quoted the following from Bernstein's *Lassalle's Reden und Schriften*, Berlin, 1893, vol. i. pp. 201 ff. This edition is referred to hereafter as "Bernstein," and Lassalle's works are throughout quoted from this edition.

defence is dangerous to public order. It is true that a few copies of my speech have been distributed against my will, but neither do I know—and the Court knows just as little—whether the copy which it received is really a copy of my speech, nor do I know at this moment whether I shall really deliver the speech as I gave it to my bookseller. Since I do not know it, and cannot know it, how will the Court make a decision on the ground of a fact which it does not know? I propose, therefore, that the Court should readmit the public.

"(The judges whisper a moment, and then reject the proposal.)

"*Lassalle* (addressing the jury in a loud voice). Well, gentlemen, then nothing remains for me but to make a solemn protest to you against the sanguinary deed of violence which has been committed here under your eyes. After six months of painful imprisonment, I am deprived of my last right, the right to brand this accusation, the right to unfold, to the astonished eyes of the citizens, the crimes, the infamies, the atrocities which are committed under the toga of a judge. (Great disturbance among the judges.) Without publicity, the right of free defence shrinks to a mere child's plaything. How, gentlemen, they dare, before your very eyes, to prolong the unworthy hypocrisy which has characterised this trial from the beginning! I am told, 'The defence is free; speak, defend yourself,' and in the same instant a gag is thrust into my mouth! I am told, 'Fight; here is a weapon,' and in the same instant my hands are tied behind me! And I am to acknowledge this infamous hypocrisy, this shameless violence, by still defending myself with closed doors?

"The excitement among the judges, in the meantime, had been growing greater and greater. The former burgomaster grew as red as a crab, and threw himself about on his chair in uncontrollable fury. The President interrupted the accused, 'You must not speak so of a decision of the Court; I shall forbid you to speak.'

" *Lassalle* (violently addressing the President). Inquisitor-in-Chief! the prisoner's dock has been from all time the refuge of free speech. You have no right to interrupt me. I will prove to you, from the annals of history, that even the chief inquisitors of Spain, when they held a public sitting, allowed the accused freely to unfold all his opinions and doubts, all that they called blasphemy against God. If the inquisitors of Spain allowed the accused the right to blaspheme against God, then it is open to me to blaspheme against the State and the Court of Assize."

The young rhetorician of twenty-three then showed in detail, with masterly logic and legal knowledge, the illegality of the President's proceedings. The President hurriedly and briefly charged the jury, and after a consultation these returned with a verdict of not guilty. The Crown then appealed to a court without a jury, where Lassalle was sentenced to six months' imprisonment. Such was, and is, Prussian justice.

Throughout the fifties Lassalle took no part in public life. He completed his work on Heraclitus, and wrote a great legal work on Acquired Rights, both of which gave him a considerable reputation in the learned world. Less commendable was a historical drama, in bad blank verse, entitled *Franz von Sickingen*. In 1859, when the attention of Europe was absorbed by Garibaldi and Louis Napoleon, he wrote an anonymous pamphlet, his first and last expression of opinion on foreign politics, entitled "The Italian War and the Duty of Prussia," in which he seems— though opinions as to its merits differ widely—to have shown at least an intimate acquaintance with foreign affairs, and a shrewd prevision of the course

which events would take. This was followed by a
paper on Fichte, in which he urged German Unity
on a Republican basis. Both here and in his more
learned works, he shows himself a thorough Hegelian; the Idea, for him, rules events, and different
historical epochs embody different phases of the
Idea. To this thorough-going Hegelianism belongs
Lassalle's worship of the State, which is often erro-
neously attributed also to Marx and his modern followers. " It is the duty and purpose of the State,"
he says on one occasion,[1] " to facilitate and effect the
great advances of mankind in civilisation. This is
its calling. For this it exists: it has always served,
and has always had to serve, for this end." In his
more thorough Hegelianism, and in this respect for
the State, lie his chief differences from Marx, and
the chief causes of the division which subsequently
arose between his followers and the orthodox Social
Democrats.

But in these writings, Lassalle was purely theoretical and scholarly. His first appearance as a
practical politician was occasioned by the *Verfas-
sungskonflikt*, or conflict about the Constitution, which
had arisen between the Crown and the Prussian
Diet. In spite of the Suffrage by three Classes,
the Progressives, in December 1861, had obtained
a majority; the King endeavoured to govern without the Chamber, and open disagreement broke out.
Under these circumstances, Lassalle was invited, in
the spring of 1862, to lecture to a Berlin liberal
association, and chose as his theme *Verfassungswesen*,
the nature of constitutions. In this lecture, Lassalle

[1] *Offenes Antwortschreiben*, vol. ii. p. 432.

explained, to the disgust of the assembled Liberals, whose tactics were to oppose the king's power by the justice and legality of their claims,—that constitutional questions are merely questions of power. Constitutions need not be written, for the law is merely the crystallised embodiment of the actual forces of the State ; in such questions might is right, and the king, since he has the army on his side, cannot be resisted by mere legal pleas. The actual forces of the State are then briefly passed in review. The king, who is obeyed by the army and the cannon, is a fragment of constitution ; a nobility, which has influence with court and king, is a fragment of constitution. The great kings of industry could cause a victorious revolt against any attempt to reintroduce guilds, therefore these are a fragment of constitution. The bankers and the Bourse are a fragment of constitution, and so, within certain limits, is public opinion. "And since your combined resistance, gentlemen, would be hard to withstand, you see that, in certain of the very extremest cases, you are all a fragment of constitution. We have now seen, gentlemen," so Lassalle sums up this argument, "what the constitution of a country is, namely, the actually existing powers and forces in the country."[1]

This lecture, though it expresses precisely the opinion of orthodox Social Democracy, was regarded by liberals and Conservatives alike as a blow to the opposition. The Governmental press was overjoyed that another former revolutionary should have seen the error of his ways, and the Progressives were

[1] *Ibid.*, vol. i. p. 481.

thoroughly disgusted. Nevertheless, Lassalle twice
repeated the same lecture, and only in November
did he see fit to develop the consequences of his
former purely academic discussion. " The princes,
gentlemen," so his first lecture had ended, " have
practical servants, not fine speakers, but practical
servants, such as you might well desire." How such
practical servants should act was the subject of his
second lecture " *Was nun ?* " " *Aussprechen das, was
ist,*" to say frankly what are the facts, and trust
to public opinion at home and abroad, was his
advice. Let the Diet refuse all further deliberation
till the king should consent to be constitutional,
and the weakening of the Government's credit would
soon force a capitulation. This advice, whether
wise or not, is typical of the peaceful but energetic
measures by which, as opposed to armed revolution,
Lassalle desired to conduct all political agitation.

More important than these two papers was Lassalle's *Arbeiterprogramm,* or Workmen's Programme,
which was first delivered to a suburban workman's
association in the spring of 1862. Though, at the
time, it seems to have attracted little attention—
chiefly owing to its strictly theoretical and scientific
form—it obtained afterwards, when published as a
pamphlet, a great hold on the more socialistic working-men, and was, indeed, the cause of the letter
from the Leipzig Committee which gave occasion
for his whole agitation.

The *Arbeiterprogramm* is in the main, as Bernstein
says, a reproduction, suited to the circumstances
of the time, of the Communist Manifesto. In its
economic doctrines, in its view of history, in its

recognition of the fourth estate as the one revolutionary factor in society, the one class whose interests govern the future, it is almost wholly Marxian; but in some important points it shows already the difference which afterwards led to so sharp a division. The materialistic view of history is not consistently worked out, and legal explanations are often substituted for economic causes. A more important difference from Marx lies in the emphasis laid on the State. The Manchester School's idea of the State, according to which it has only to protect men's persons and property, is a "night-watchman idea, for it can only imagine the State as a night-watchman, whose whole function consists in preventing robbery and housebreaking"[1] The true function of the State is to "help the development of the human race towards freedom," to effect those steps which all, as individuals, must desire, but which no single individual can effect. But this function can only be fulfilled by a State which adequately represents the interests of all, by a State, that is, with equal and universal suffrage. In the present State, the invention of machinery and the growth of the factory system have made the wage-earners the *actually* most powerful class; it is therefore natural and necessary to make them *legally* the most powerful, by abolishing the property vote, and introducing a pure democracy. Economic progress has already brought the revolution of which this would only be the legal recognition; for "it is impossible to *make* a revolution; it is only possible to recognise legally and carry out consistently a revolu-

[1] Bernstein, vol. ii. p. 45.

tion which has already taken place in the actual conditions of a society." [1] In this sense, Arkwright's cotton-spinning machine was a revolution.[2] " To wish to *make* a revolution is the folly of immature people, who know nothing of the laws of history " [3] The French Revolution was the revolution of the bourgeoisie against the feudal nobility, of industry against landed property ; the revolution which began in 1848, which it is the political function of the working classes to advance, is the revolution of the wage-earning proletariat against the rule of the great capitalists. But unlike former class-victories, the victory of the proletariat, of the disinherited, since they have no privileges to rescue, is the victory of all mankind, its freedom is the freedom of the human race itself, its rule is the rule of all. " The high world-historical importance of this mission must absorb all your thoughts. The vices of the oppressed become you no longer, nor the idle dissipations of the thoughtless, nor even the harmless frivolities of the unimportant. You are the rock on which the Church of the present must be built " [4]

The power and logical development of this programme are those of the Communist Manifesto, and its applicability to the time depends, like Marx's whole political system, on the previous development of society to the capitalistic form. Unfortunately for Lassalle's agitation, this development was, in Germany, very far indeed from complete. The opposition of labour and capital, as the very name of the association to which Lassalle was speaking

---

[1] Bernstein, vol. ii. p. 22.
[2] *Ibid.*, p. 23.
[3] *Ibid.*, p. 22.
[4] *Ibid.*, p. 48.

—the Oranienburg Handicraftsmen's Association—should have suggested to him, was by no means so well developed as to give any chance of success to a movement of the industrial wage-earners alone. More than half the population of Prussia was engaged in agriculture; of the town workers, many were engaged in handicrafts, and only about 10 per cent. of the population were dependent for their livelihood on factories.[1] The policy, which had been suggested to Marx and Engels by the more advanced industry of England, could, consequently, have no chance of immediate success in Germany.   Lassalle was therefore forced, in his later agitatioh, in spite of his theories, to try to *make* a revolution : not by rousing the people to armed insurrection, but by the simpler and rapider method of converting Bismarck and the Prussian Ministry.   This policy the later Socialists have always avoided, as treachery to their class, but by avoiding it, they have lost all hope, for the moment, of directly bringing about any one of the reforms which they demand.

The *Arbeiterprogramm*, in the form of a pamphlet, obtained a wide popularity among the more advanced workmen, many of whom had begun to feel the insufficiency of Schulze-Delitzsch's programme.   The men of Leipzig, who were among the most advanced, sent a deputation to Berlin, in October 1862, to make a final attempt at co-operation with the Progressives. The three men who constituted the deputation were all Socialists, and the attempt at reconciliation failed, as was expected.   After the return of the deputation to Leipzig, a resolution was passed to invite Lassalle

[1] See Bernstein's " Lassalle," footnote, vol. i. p. 126.

to express, in any form which he might think fit, his opinion of the movement, of the policy it should pursue, and of the value of the associations. There must exist, they thought, " other ways and means, besides those recommended by Schulze-Delitzsch, for attaining the ends of the workman's movement, namely, improvement of the condition of the working-men politically, materially, and mentally ; " and owing to the great value of Lassalle's brochure, they attached a high importance to his opinion on these points.[1]

To this invitation Lassalle replied, on the 1st March, by the *Offenes Antwortschreiben*, or public letter of reply, in which he set forth, clearly and succinctly, the policy which, in his opinion, a workmen's movement should follow. They had discussed whether they should abstain from politics or join the Progressives. He would urge them to a third alternative ; they should take part in politics, but as a separate independent labour-party. Schulze-Delitzsch's friendly societies could only benefit individuals, for as soon as all took part in them, wages would fall, by that iron law which keeps labourers at the bare minimum of subsistence. The one and only way of overcoming this iron law was to abolish the capitalist, by establishing associations for co-operative production. In this way the gains of the undertaker would fall to the workman ; but no industrial undertaking could succeed nowadays without large capital, and where were the workmen to get this capital ? The only way to get it was by State credit ; let the State lend them the money at the

[1] Bernstein, vol. i. pp. 114-116.

normal rate of interest, and then they would be
able to compete with private capital on equal terms.
But how determine the State to this undertaking?
Obviously it would not be possible in a State
governed by capitalists; they must agitate, therefore, for universal suffrage, and then the State would
become the true and faithful image of the will of
the people. What workmen had to do, for the
present, therefore, was to form a universal association throughout Germany, on the analogy of the
Anti-Corn-Law League, with the one and only aim
of obtaining universal suffrage. This achieved, they
could establish the productive associations and
destroy the Iron Law. They need not distrust the
State, for what was the State but the great association of the working classes? Seventy-two and a
quarter per cent. of the families of Prussia had an
annual income under 100 thaler (£15); eighty-nine
per cent. had an income under 200 thaler (£30).
The State, therefore, *was* the poorest classes: State-
help was only help from the great national association for the smaller associations; why then should
they fear it? The universal association, therefore,
must organise a legal and peaceful, but unwearying
agitation for the one single purpose of universal suffrage. "Look neither to the right nor to the left; be
deaf to everything which is not direct and universal
suffrage, or can be brought into connection with it
and lead to it! . . . The universal suffrage of 89 to
96 per cent. of the population, regarded as a hunger-
question, and spread through the whole body of the
nation with the keenness of hunger—be quite un-
concerned, gentlemen, there is no power which can

long withstand that! This is the token that you must set up. This .is the token in which you will conquer! There is no other for you!" [1]

At the time when this was written, the struggle between the Government and the Diet was at its height. The air was full of threats of revolution, and it seemed a doubtful question which party would conquer. The Government had already made attempts to sow dissension among the Liberals, and especially to detach the working classes by promises of State-help. Lassalle's advice appeared to the Liberals, therefore, a traitorous overture to the Government, and as such, was bitterly attacked. Many workmen's associations held aloof from the new movement. The Liberals denied Lassalle's Iron Law, but in an able debating speech, at Leipzig, he quoted Say, Ricardo, Adam Smith, Mill, Rau, and Roscher, to prove that it was held by all economists of repute. After this they changed their tactics, and maintained that the Iron Law was a law of nature, which no institutions could alter. Here, again, Lassalle had an easy controversial victory. In two great speeches at Frankfort, he persuaded the local associations to pass a resolution in favour of his Universal Association, and on May 23rd, it was founded at Leipzig, in the presence of delegates from ten towns, among which Berlin was not represented. The statutes, which Lassalle drew up himself, gave him, as president, dictatorial power; this was done partly to avoid the Coalition Laws by strict centralisation, partly to satisfy Lassalle's ambition and belief in the power of an individual will.

[1] Bernstein, vol. ii. p. 445.

The Association grew slowly, and Lassalle's energy, which was immense but sporadic, soon gave out. Early in July he left Germany for his health, but continued to direct the agitation by letter. Three months after its foundation, the Association numbered only 900 members, and Berlin still held aloof. For Lassalle, who had confidently expected, within a year, to organise the whole of the German working classes, this was a bitter disappointment. He began to look for more rapid means of victory, and when he returned in September, he adopted a new tone. With more bitterness against the Liberals, he combined a flattering attitude towards the Government : Bismarck was a man, he said, while the Progressives were a lot of old women. He also began to exaggerate enormously the results of his agitation, which, in spite of the immense personal enthusiasm which he aroused, remained without any very solid result. He made a great effort to win Berlin, first by an address "To the workmen of Berlin," then by meetings and speeches. In the beginning he had some success, and obtained 200 Berlin members, but by February 1864 this number had sunk to three dozen. People suspected him for his bitter attack on the Liberals, and still more, probably, for the negotiations with Bismarck, which he carried on throughout the winter. What occurred in these interviews it seems impossible to discover with certainty ; probably he sought to win Bismarck to universal suffrage and to State credit for his co-operative associations. The Liberals, since they obtained such good majorities by the three-classes system, were very lukewarm about reform of the

suffrage, while the Government, relying on the Conservative instincts of the agrarian population, had
serious thoughts of a change. Bismarck did, in
fact, grant universal suffrage three years later, and
this may, to some extent, justify Lassalle's *tactics;*
but the increased Conservatism of the popular representatives seems to have shown Bismarck's states-
manship, and throws great doubt on the wisdom of
Lassalle's *programme.* Bismarck himself gave a most
interesting, though not wholly reliable account of
these interviews, in the Reichstag fifteen years
later.[1]

" Lassalle himself wished urgently to enter into negotiations with me, and if I could find time to search among old
papers, I believe I could yet find the letter in which the
wish is expressed, and in which reasons are given why I
should allow the wish to be fulfilled.   Nor did I make
it difficult for Lassalle to meet me.   I saw him, and from
the time that I first spoke an hour with him, I have not
regretted it.   I did not see him three or four times a week,
but only three or four times altogether.   Our relations
could not have the nature of political negotiations.   For
what could Lassalle offer or give me?   He had nothing
behind him, and in all political negotiations the *Do ut des*
lies in the background, even though, for the sake of decorum,
one may not say so.   If I were to have said to myself :
' What have you, poor devil, to give ?' he had nothing which
he could have given me as Minister ; but what he had was
something which attracted me extraordinarily as a private
man.   He was one of the most intellectual and gifted men
with whom I have ever had intercourse, a man who was
ambitious on a grand scale, but by no means a Republican ;
he had very decided national and monarchical sympathies ;

[1] Speech in the Reichstag, September 16, 1878.

the idea which he strove to realise was the German Empire, and in that we had a point of contact. Lassalle was extremely ambitious, and it was perhaps a matter of doubt to him whether the German Empire would end with the Hohenzollern or the Lassalle dynasty; but he was monarchical through and through. . . . Our conversations lasted hours, and I was always sorry when they came to an end. There was no talk of negotiations, for during our conversation I could scarcely get in a word."

Whether there were negotiations or not, it is certain that Lassalle, in his speeches, began to promise more and more confidently that the Government would grant universal suffrage, and it is a proof of his anti-democratic disposition, that he regarded such a result as equally satisfactory with a suffrage won by popular agitation. "Bismarck," he wrote on one occasion, "is only my plenipotentiary," and he undoubtedly intended only to use him so long as he should be useful. But this policy required, as Bismarck said, that Lassalle should be a considerable power, and necessitated the most reckless exaggeration of his actual achievements. Since these remained small, Lassalle became more and more Bismarck's plenipotentiary; instead of being the master, he became the tool, and this situation led to ever greater outward boasting and inward discouragement. In his last tour of agitation, in May 1864, which has been described as a triumphal progress more like that of a monarch than that of a private citizen, he spoke much of promises from the king, of the benevolence of the Prussian Government, and of the weakness of the Liberal Party, which he stigmatised as a mere clique. But the speeches of this

time no longer show the old vigour, or the old
straightforward logic; the tendency to demagogy,
which had hitherto been subordinate, now became
supreme, and was only varied by unmeasured self-
laudation. He was disappointed and broken in
health, and vainly endeavoured to conceal his weakness by pompous boasts. He seems to have felt that
his strength could not hold out much longer. " If
I am set aside," so ends the last of his great speeches,
" may some avenger and successor arise out of my
bones ! May this powerful national movement of
civilisation not fall with my person, but may the
conflagration which I have kindled spread farther
and farther, so long as a single one of you still
breathes ! Promise me this, and as a sign, hold up
your right hands ! "

Soon after this, Lassalle went to Switzerland for
his health, and was killed in a foolish and conven-
tional duel.

It is almost impossible, on first reading the history
of Lassalle's agitation, not to wonder in what its
great importance consists. Barely a dozen great
speeches, three or four brilliant defences in Court,
a few pamphlets and a very few followers—that, at
first sight, seems to sum up Lassalle's achievements.
What he really did, however, lay not in the immediate results, but in his emotional effect on men's
minds, in the forcible attention which his supremely
dramatic appearance demanded and obtained from
the whole nation. He *forced* men, even against their
wills, to reflect on their political circumstances, and
see them as they were. " The name of Lassalle,"
says Bernstein, " grew to be a banner for which the

masses became more and more enthusiastic, the more Lassalle's writings penetrated among the people. Designed for immediate effect, written with extraordinary talent, popular and yet emphasising theoretic points of view, they exercised, and in part still exercise to-day, a great missionary effect. The *Arbeiterprogramm* (Workmen's Programme), the *Offenes Antwortschreiben* (Public Letter of Reply), the *Arbeiterlesebuch* (Workmen's Primer), &c., have won hundreds of thousands to Socialism. The force of conviction, which runs through these writings, has inflamed hundreds of thousands to the fight for the rights of labour"[1] "Where there was, in general, only undetermined desire, he spread conscious endeavour, he brought home to German labour the recognition of its social mission, he taught it to organise itself as an independent political party, and in this way accelerated, by years at least, the development of the movement"[2]

That Lassalle practically created the German labour movement, that it long bore, and still bears in part, the stamp of his personality, is indubitable. Whether the path on which he led it was wise, whether his programme or his tactics were likely to benefit the working classes, is a different and more difficult question.

As regards his programme, it is noticeable that his theoretical economics, like those of Marx, assumed absolute free competition, and therefore coincided almost entirely with those of the Manchester School. Granted this postulate, his theory is generally orthodox and wholly unoriginal. Owing partly,

[1] Bernstein, vol. i. p. 182.   [2] *Ibid.*, p. 185.

no doubt, to the hurry with which most of his work was done, he seldom made acknowledgments of his sources; his theoretic Socialism, however, seems to have been a combination of Marx and Rodbertus. Rodbertus was a country gentleman and practical agriculturist, who advocated a Conservative Socialism which became the parent of the German State Socialists. His economic theory was almost wholly in agreement with that of Marx; it committed the same mistakes, but was not redeemed by the same brilliancy. Like Marx, Rodbertus never understood the difference between landlord and farmer. The practical measures, however, which his theory led him to advocate, were very different from those proclaimed by Marx. He was not a democrat, and he *was* a patriot. He wished the labourer's condition to be improved, but from above, not by the labourer himself. In spite of his economically thoroughgoing Socialism in short, he was politically a Conservative, a landlord, and a Prussian.[1]

[1] The importance of Rodbertus, in the development of Socialism, is a disputed point, on which there has been much hot controversy between Marxians and State Socialists. The latter have even maintained, as Rodbertus himself maintained, that Marx shamelessly plagiarised him. For this view there seems, however, absolutely no evidence. (See George Adler, *Die Grundlagen der Karl Marx'-schen Kritik*, p. 196). That Rodbertus has great importance in the development of general theoretic Socialism, and that he greatly influenced Lassalle's views on economics, is certain. At the same time, his specifically political importance lies, in my opinion, more with the State Socialists than with Social Democracy. For those points in which Lassalle differed from Marx and agreed with Rodbertus, were not taken up permanently by his followers, and have to-day disappeared, almost without a trace, from the party programme and the party opinion. On these grounds, and not because I hold Rodbertus in himself unimportant, I thought it advisable to treat him very lightly in a history of Social Democracy.

The point in which Lassalle's practical economic
programme differed from both these authorities,
namely the proposal of co-operative associations, was
severely criticised, in a series of letters to Lassalle, by
Rodbertus, who, partly for this reason, and partly
because he disapproved of an Independent Labour
Party, always held aloof from the agitation. The
criticisms of Rodbertus are, in the main, the same as
those of later Socialists : that the associations would,
in their turn, become competing capitalists ; that
those who, from the nature of their occupations,
could not join any association, would form a fifth
estate as miserable as the present proletariat ; that
there would be no guarantee against over-production,
which is, according to Rodbertus and Marx, the cause
of financial crises ; and finally, that the transition
from such societies to the collectivist state would be
difficult, if not impossible. These objections, it must
be admitted, are in the main sound, and it is a gain
to Social Democracy to have eliminated Lassalle's
scheme from its programme. Against the Iron Law
it must be urged that, apart from the Malthusian
limitation of population, it can be suspended by a
sudden extension of industry and consequent increase
of the demand for labour, or by Trade Unions. This,
though not sufficiently emphasised by Marx, is now
recognised by the leaders of Social Democracy ; the
small interest which the people take in Trade Unions,
however, and the preponderatingly political character
of the German Labour Movement, are still traceable, in
part, to the mistaken influence of Lassalle's Iron Law.
The phrase Iron Law is misleading, for not only does
Lassalle admit that what are regarded as necessaries

may vary from time to time, according to the standard of comfort, but like Rodbertus, he uses wages—as do most Socialists, though often unconsciously—in the Ricardian sense of the *proportion* of produce which falls to labour. In this sense, increase of productivity, unless accompanied by a proportional increase of absolute wages, appears as a fall in wages, since it diminishes the labourer's proportion—a consequence which Lassalle, following Rodbertus, exploits to the uttermost.

As to Lassalle's tactics, though it is almost impossible to estimate their wisdom, it is easy to see that many grave objections can be urged against them. In the conflict about the Constitution, the Liberal party was fighting a real if half-hearted battle for freedom and progress, and an Independent Labour Party, if it were to exist at all, would have been much more likely to achieve success by a conditional support of Liberalism than by playing into the hands of the Government. Also Lassalle underestimated, throughout his whole career, the reactionary forces among the people themselves. When he proved triumphantly that 89 per cent. of the population belonged to the poorest classes, he forgot how many of these were engaged in agriculture and handicrafts, and how few belonged to the revolutionary class of wage-earners. This was a heritage from the Communist Manifesto, but Lassalle, who had lived all his life in Prussia, ought to have known better the conditions of his own country. A class which is still a small minority cannot hope to win much from democracy, and in this respect, Bismarck showed himself a shrewder politician than Lassalle. The time when Universal Suffrage or an Independent Labour Party could lead to the establishment of Socialism, especially by the peaceful means which Lassalle always advocated, was still far distant, as is proved by the subsequent history of Social Democracy.

But whether universal suffrage was a wise demand or not, it seems certain that Lassalle's method, of confining the whole agitation to one point, was a wise one, and that the later movement, by demanding its whole programme at once, has lost much of the influence on politics which it might otherwise have had. By a man of Lassalle's force of character, with more patience of slow results, such an agitation might undoubtedly have been successfully carried out. But Lassalle's ungovernable will, and his incapacity to realise that it could be resisted, led him into a situation from which his sudden death was perhaps a fortunate deliverance. "The disease which killed him," says Brandes,[1] "was an arrogant will, as others die of too great a heart. But the will or the self-confidence, whose excess killed him, was also the principle which upheld him throughout his life. He stands out in history as a monument of will."

[1] *Ferdinand Lassalle: ein litterarisches Charakterbild*, 3rd ed., Leipzig, 1894, p. 174.

LECTURE III

LASSALLE'S sudden death threw the affairs of his
small but enthusiastic following into the greatest
confusion, and produced a feeling of extreme con-
sternation among the members of the Universal
Association. Some ardent worshippers refused to
believe that he was dead; most regarded his death
as the result of deep-laid governmental plots. That
he, their great inspired leader, should be killed in
an ordinary duel about a love-affair, seemed quite
inconceivable. Among some, whose interest in the
movement was really an interest in Lassalle, a complete Lassalle-religion was developed; all his words
were treasured, and the letter of his policy was
strictly followed. The larger section of the Association, however, following Bernhard Becker, whom
Lassalle had appointed as his successor, gradually,
though half-heartedly, admitted the utility of Trade
Unions, and passed beyond Lassalle's actual words.
Becker was an incompetent leader, who imitated
Lassalle's faults without possessing his genius. The
unmeasured boasting which, in the master, was more
or less justified by his real force, became, in the

disciple, the most ridiculous exaggeration. " I alone among you represent revolution, and have revolutionary power in me," he said on one occasion ; and this arrogance was accompanied by the most insolent disregard of others, and the most irritating use of his dictatorship.

Under Becker's mismanagement the Association, small as it had been before, lost ground everywhere. In 1867, however, he was replaced by v. Schweitzer, a man of great ability, and an intimate friend of Lassalle. Schweitzer rapidly improved the affairs of the Association. Thus, by a bold agitation in 1869, he succeeded in obtaining a footing in Berlin, which had been, since Lassalle's failure, an impregnable stronghold of the Progressives.[1] He had understood and known Lassalle's policy more thoroughly than any of his contemporaries—too thoroughly, perhaps, for by his support of Bismarck he became universally suspected. The organ of the Association, which he edited and rigidly controlled, published in 1867 a series of articles entitled " The Bismarck Ministry," which disgusted all sound Democrats, and caused Marx, Engels, and Liebknecht, who were on the staff, publicly to withdraw their names. Again, in 1867, Schweitzer stood in Elberfeld against Bismarck and a Liberal. Having been defeated himself in the first ballot, he ordered his followers to vote for Bismarck, who was thus enabled to defeat the Liberal candidate.[2] Whether true or false, it was and is, the opinion of all thorough Socialists that he had become in fact, if not in form, a traitor and

---

[1] Mehring, *Die Deutsche Sozialdemokratie*, 3rd ed., p. 123.
[2] *Ibid.*, p. 84.

a Government agent. At the general meeting in
1869, Bebel and Liebknecht were invited to be
present, and prevailed on the Association to adopt
a more democratic organisation, and a more socialistic programme. Hereupon Schweitzer made a
coup d'état, restored the old "democratic dictatorship," as he called it, and refused to print any
adverse criticisms in his paper. A large number of
dissentients, in consequence, left the Association.
" When Herr v. Schweitzer dictates," they said in a
formal protest, " the members have simply to obey,
and yet they are still called the 'sovereign people.'
No greater mockery has ever been offered to any
human being." Even among the remaining members, a growing opposition made itself felt, and
finally, after he had been elected to the Reichstag
by the help of Conservative votes, Schweitzer was
forced to resign the presidency of the Association in
July 1871, and was soon afterwards expelled from
it as a traitor. From this time on, the fanatical
worship of Lassalle, and adherence to his whole
policy, rapidly decayed. Marx's influence, as represented by Bebel and Liebknecht, made itself more
and more felt, and in 1875 the Association amalga-
mated with the "honourable" Social Democrats, as
they called themselves, the party of thorough-going
Marxian Communism.

To trace the growth of this Marxian party, which
to-day exclusively represents German Democratic
Socialism, we must for a moment return to London,
which was throughout the centre of Marx's influence.
This influence, as we have seen, began with the
Communist League, though the German police, in

a priceless passage of the "Black Book," succeeded in tracing it back, in a most lucid manner, to Baboeuf and the infernal machine.[1] From Baboeuf this document proceeds to Mazzini, who, according to its account, founded a "young Italy." This, the police explain, gave rise to a "young Germany," a "young France," a "young Poland," &c. All these combined into a "young Europe," whose purpose was the "Overthrow of the old Europe." This gave rise to the "League of the Despised," which already had communistic tendencies; object: U iiversal Overthrow. The "League of the Despised" produced "The League of the Just;" object: Universal Overthrow. Out of this developed, in the course of time, the "Communist League," which, we are informed, was "founded in London in the forties out of members of all older conspiracies in Germany, France, Italy, and Poland." So far the police: for my part, I have no knowledge of these pre-Adamite transgressions, and am content to regard the Communist League as primary and original sin. The Communist League was a small society of propagandists, and Marx's Manifesto, though it long remained little known, was read by many young members who afterwards became important agitators. In consequence of this work, and of the "Critique of Political Economy," Marx was invited, in 1864, to present an address to a newly-constituted society, the International Working-Men's Association. This Association, the subject of so much mystery and

[1] *Hochverraths-Prozess wider Liebknecht, Bebel und Hepner*, Berlin, 1895, p. 64. This book is referred to, in what follows, as *Hochverraths-Prozess*.

melodrama, which contained revolutionaries of all countries—English, French, Germans, Italians, and Poles,—held its inaugural meeting at St. Martin's Hall in September 1864, with Professor Beesley in the chair. It was doubtful, at first, whether Marx or Mazzini would lead the Association, but Marx, by a very able address, won the inaugural meeting to his views, and obtained the privilege of drawing up the statutes and programme. Mazzini, who was by no means a Socialist, resigned with all his Italian followers, and thus left Marx supreme. At the first general meeting in Geneva, two years later, Marx's statutes were accepted. The programme was essentially the same as that of the Communist Manifesto, with a strong emphasis on the need of internationalism, while the organisation allowed any socialistic associations to affiliate, and decreed an Annual Congress. Like almost every Socialist organisation, it soon lost an anarchist contingent, which followed the Russian Bakunin, and became the parent of modern nihilism. Nevertheless, the International remained very powerful, and succeeded in establishing Socialistic movements in almost all countries of Europe, and also in the United States, in which country alone it still formally exists. Marx, emerging, at the periodical Congresses, from his scholarly retirement, retained his power, though with some difficulty, and increased his prestige immensely by the publication of his "Capital" in 1867. Although the German Laws forbade the formal affiliation of German Associations, the principles of the International gradually gained ground, and Marx's works, in the original or in a popularised

form, were studied with growing admiration by all
the leaders of workmen's organisations. We must
now confine ourselves to Germany, and trace, more
in detail, the means by which Marx's influence and
the principles of the International were spread.

Lassalle's agitation, though it had not obtained
many actual followers—at his death, the Association
only numbered 4610 members—had succeeded in
the primary object of an agitation, in that it had
agitated everybody. Already in 1863, very soon
after the founding of the Association, a number of
Arbeiterbildungs-Vereine, or societies for workmen's
education—which, in spite of their name, were
really political—combined, as supporters of Schulze-
Delitzsch, into a league of German workmen's
societies, to oppose Lassalle from the side of Liberalism. Their headquarters were at Leipzig, and here
Bebel, from the first one of their most important
members, and at that time an adherent of the Progressive party, became acquainted with Liebknecht.
Through Liebknecht's influence, combined with the
banal and foolish opposition offered by official
Liberalism to the new movement, he was gradually
converted to Socialism. Already in 1865, Bebel,
who is an extremely powerful orator, succeeded in
winning the Saxon contingent to Socialistic principles, and in 1868, when he was president of the
League, he and Liebknecht persuaded the annual
Congress to accept, by a large majority, the most
important items in the programme of the International. The minority declared that such programmes were mere phrases, that their demands
could not be attained within measurable time, and

that reliance on the State weakened the spirit of self-help, from which alone a solution of the social question was to be expected. They drew up a formal protest, and left the League. This loss, however, was made good by the dissentient members of the Universal Association, who found here a more congenial atmosphere than under Schweitzer's dictatorship. Finally, in 1869, at a Congress of all German-speaking Socialists in Eisenach, the League formally dissolved, and after a fruitless attempt at union with the Universal Association, it formed, with the German members of the International, the Social Democratic Workmen's Party, afterwards known as the Eisenach or "honourable" party, which recognised the principles of the International, and declared itself, so far as the laws allowed, affiliated to that organisation.

The chief agent in this rapid development was Liebknecht, who, though not himself a great orator, succeeded in winning, by his strong conviction and scholarly education, the powerful oratorical support of August Bebel. In a trial for high treason, the result of his opposition to the annexation of Alsace-Lorraine, Liebknecht gave an interesting autobiography, which greatly helps to explain the success of his persistent efforts to spread Socialistic principles in Germany.

"Arising from a family of small officials," he says, "I was destined by my relations for office life. But already at school I learnt to know the writings of Saint-Simon, which opened a new world to me. For a bread-and-butter study I had in any case no inclination. At the age of sixteen I entered the university, and studied the most various subjects. I dived into this and that, like every student who really wishes to learn, and is not confined to the strait-waistcoat of a bread-and-butter study. I soon abandoned finally the thought of entering the service of the State, as it was not compatible with my political and social opinions. But for a while I cherished the plan of becoming a *Privat-dozent*, and of perhaps obtaining a professorship in one of the smaller, more independent universities. I did not long deceive myself, however, with this vain delusion. I became persuaded that, without sacrificing my principles, I had not the slightest prospect of obtaining the teacher's certificate, and therefore resolved, in 1847, to emigrate to America. I carried out the necessary preparations without delay, and was already on the journey to a seaport, when I made the acquaintance, by accident, of a man who had a position as teacher in Switzerland. He disapproved of my plan, and referring to the changes imminent, to all appearance, in European conditions, advised me with such persuasive words to cross into republican Switzerland, that I turned back at the next post station, and, instead of Hamburg, I went to Zurich. . . . I visited the German Workman's Association in Zurich for the sake of instruction, as I had opportunity here, for the first time, to hear the workmen themselves discuss their situation and their aims. . . . On the 23rd of February 1848 came the news of the beginning of the fight in Paris. My dearest hopes were now fulfilled, for I did not doubt the victory of the people. I could not endure to stay any longer in Switzerland. I took a hasty adieu of my circle of friends, and two hours later I was already on the way to Paris. In spite of my haste, the fight was ended, and the barricades were already in part removed when I reached my goal; yet my hopes had not deceived me,—the July Throne had fallen. . . . The effects of the revolution on Germany are still fresh in our memories. I did not doubt that it was possible to realise the idea of a German republic, . . . but unfortunately I grew ill in Paris from over-exertion, and could not co-operate in the end of the fight. . . . I returned to Zurich, to my old studies. But only for a few months. In the end of September Struve unfurled the banner of the Republic. At his call, I crossed the Rhine with a dozen like-minded companions, and we succeeded in bringing together, within three days, a fairly strong corps of volunteers. But when I reached Lauffenburg, where all the volunteer corps were to be concentrated, I heard the news that Struve had been defeated and taken prisoner. I made an attempt to reach my corps. The attempt failed; I was taken prisoner, and had to spend three-quarters of a year under arrest during investigation. At the end of this time I was set free without a trial. . . . I took part as journalist and soldier in the campaign to secure a constitution for the Empire. We fought for a free united Germany, and the Prussian army, commanded by the present Emperor of Germany (Wilhelm I.), suppressed the movement, and restored the old division and bondage. I escaped to Switzerland, and sought to win the German Workmen's Associations of Switzerland, whose membership was at that time very large, for a united organisation and a strictly Socialist programme. A Congress was called to Murten. The Swiss Federal Council pretended to believe that the real purpose of the Congress was an invasion of Baden, and arrested all the delegates, including myself. . . . I was banished from Switzerland by command of the Federal Council, and delivered to the French authorities, who sent me, with a passport of compulsion, to London. In London I became a member of the Communist League. The only member of the League whom I had previously known was Engels, whom I had met in Geneva. Marx I only learnt to know in London. . . . From the Communist Manifesto, which is to be regarded as the programme of the Communist League, it is as clear as noonday that this much maligned association was revolutionary, it is true, in that it aimed at a complete transformation of social and political conditions, but that, just because it held revolution to be an organic process, it was free from, and even hostile to, every sort of mechanical revolution-mongery, since in the development of society unalterable laws hold good, which must be investigated, but which only a fool could think of trying to change. . . . In London I lived thirteen years, engaged in political and social studies, and still more in the struggle for existence. In the middle of 1862, I was invited by August Brass, the red republican of '48, to join the staff of his new Berlin paper, the *Norddeutsche Allgemeine Zeitung.* I had been enabled by the amnesty, in the meantime, to return to Germany. . . . At first all went well. But after a short time, in the end of September 1862, Bismarck came into power, and I soon noticed that a change was taking place in the attitude of the paper. . . . The grounds of suspicion multiplied, and I at last obtained the proofs that Brass had bound himself to Bismarck as his literary menial. It is obvious that I had now to sever my connection with this paper, although I thereby renounced my only means of subsistence. At that time, and later, repeated attempts were made to buy me also. . . . Herr von, now Prince, Bismarck takes not only money, but people, wherever he finds them. It is indifferent to him to what party a man belongs. He even prefers apostates, for an apostate is stripped of his honour, and is therefore a passive tool in the hands of his master. The Prussian ministry was extremely anxious, at that time, to find a set-off against the unruly bourgeoisie. It wished to crush them between aristocracy and proletariat as between two millstones, according to the recipe given thirty years ago by the English Tory chief, Disraeli; for even in this point the policy of Herr von Bismarck was not original. The *Norddeutsche Allgemeine Zeitung* was repeatedly put at the disposal of myself and my friends for articles of an extreme socialistic, even communistic, tendency. I need not say that I did not allow myself to be misused for the purposes of this sordid game, and rejected with proper scorn the attempts at corruption of

Herr von Bismarck's agents. . . . In the year 1863 Lassalle began his pioneer agitation. At first I held aloof, till the shameful attacks of the bourgeois press on the young socialistic movement made it my duty of honour to forget all my scruples. I became a member of his Universal German Working-Men's Association. True to the policy already described, the governing aristocracy sought to gain control of the new labour movement. After Lassalle's sudden death, the Association unfortunately fell into the hands of men who gave assistance to these reactionary endeavours, partly from incapacity, partly from intention. This forced me to abandon my hitherto reserved behaviour, and combat openly this governmental socialism. I showed that a one-sided procedure against the bourgeoisie could only be of service to the aristocracy, that the contemplated universal suffrage, without freedom of the press, of meeting, and of combination, was nothing but an instrument of the reaction, and that "State-help" from a government of lordlings could only be granted to corrupt the workmen and make them useful for the purposes of the reaction. . . . The persecutions of the police redoubled. . . . And one fine morning I was given notice that I must leave Berlin and the State of Prussia." . . . [1]

By this banishment, Liebknecht was forced to settle in Leipzig, which, as we have seen, was Bebel's home, and the headquarters of the League of German Workmen's Societies. Thus he was enabled, by the kindly help of the police, to acquire that influence over Bebel and his followers, by which they were led, finally, to agreement with the principles of Marx and the International. The hold which Marx's principles thus gained on the German labour movement has since then continually increased. No sooner was his "Capital" published than the more

---

[1] *Hochverraths-Prozess*, pp. 67 ff.

intelligent and educated members of the party, in innumerable pamphlets and speeches, set to work to popularise his doctrines. The law of concentration of capital appealed to all town workmen, who could see, in their daily life, the rapid progress of large factories and the rapid decay of the handicrafts. The doctrine that this law, by an inherent and fatal necessity, *must* bring about the advent of the Collectivist State, inspired all the disciples with confidence of ultimate success, and gave to the future, for which they were striving, the air of a proved scientific fact, instead of the wild and visionary Utopia which it had hitherto seemed. "What cannot be reached artificially," says one of these Marxian popular pamphlets [1] "by any proposal, by any possible means, *that* the law of development of capitalistic production brings about of itself, *without any intention*. People may wish it or not, this development will be completed. This is no *plan* which some one proposes, no measure to be followed, but a pitiless insight into the nature of things."

Thus all went well for the development of Marxian principles. By the granting of universal suffrage for the North German League, the Socialists of both parties were able together to elect six members to the North German Reichstag. A great help in agitation was gained, in 1868, by the foundation of Trade Unions. These have been from the start political in spirit—at first, indeed, they were of three opposing factions, corresponding to the Marxians, Lassalleans, and Progressives. The Marxian Unions were the stronger and more numerous, but unlike

[1] W. Bracke, junior, *Der Lassalle'sche Vorschlag*, Brunswick, 1873.

our English Unions, they were founded from above, with a mainly political purpose, and a centralised organisation for the various trades, and were not a spontaneous movement of the working-men themselves. But by the conduct of the Eisenach or Marxian party during the Franco-Prussian War— one of the most honourable facts in their whole history, by the way—the growth of their principles received a severe check, so severe that, to this day, all other parties dwell with horrified pleasure on the wickedness of the Socialist attitude at that time. As followers of the International, which recognised no distinction of country, the Eisenach party could not approve of the war, and could not share the national enthusiasm which took possession of Germany. As Republicans, their sympathies, after Sedan had brought about the French Republic, were rather with France than with their own country. They urged a cheap peace, without annexation of Alsace-Lorraine, and were regarded, in consequence, as traitors to the Fatherland. Bebel, Liebknecht, and Hepner (the editor of the party organ) were arrested on a charge of high treason ; Hepner was acquitted, after fifteen months' imprisonment without trial, but Bebel and Liebknecht received sentences of two years nine months and two years respectively. Consistently with their Communist principles, they had declared their sympathy with the Paris Commune, which was largely directed, though not instigated, by the International. Whatever was told of its horrors, they regarded as bourgeois fabrications. By this declaration, also, they shocked irrevocably the moral sense of the ordinary German Philistine.

" It was," Bismarck said in introducing the Socialist law, "from the moment when, in the assembled Reichstag, either Bebel or Liebknecht, in pathetic appeal, held up the French Commune as a model of political institutions, and openly confessed before the nation the gospel of the Paris murderers and incendiaries, that I first experienced a full conviction of the danger which threatened us. That appeal to the Commune was a ray of light upon the matter, and from that moment I regarded the Social Democratic factions as an enemy against which the State and society must arm themselves." Bismarck's feelings were shared by all patriotic Germans, and the Social Democrats everywhere lost ground. Liebknecht lost his seat, and Bebel alone represented the Eisenach party in the Reichstag. Schweitzer's followers, who were national and patriotic, attacked the Eisenach party in the streets of Leipzig, and the police, for once, had to afford protection to the Social Democrats. The universal horror with which they were regarded is amusingly illustrated by an anecdote which Liebknecht tells of his experience in the Reichstag.[1] His alphabetical neighbour in the cloak-room, seeing that Liebknecht had, by accident, a cane with a little lead knob, immediately bought an out-and-out shillelagh, which kept watch over his cane to the end of the session. To this day in Germany, educated and uneducated, professors and soldiers, make it the greatest crime of Social Democracy that it refused to share in the brutal and blundering sin by which Alsace-Lorraine was annexed.

[1] *Hochverraths-Prozess*, p. 14.

Another crime of the Socialists was their vain protest against Prussian supremacy in the new German Empire. Though all democrats and revolutionaries had wished ardently for German unity, no enlightened democrat could welcome such a unity with Prussia at its head—Prussia, which, as Lassalle, though himself a Prussian, had said, stood far behind almost every other German state.[1]

Although, largely in order to gain the help of the Democracy in establishing German unity, universal suffrage was granted to all Germany, the ascendency of Prussia almost outweighed this gain. To understand the small value of the suffrage and the great evil of Prussian rule, we must, however, first make a short survey of the German Constitution as determined at Versailles after the war.

There are two ways of describing a Constitution: the pedantic way, which gives an account of the written or theoretical powers of various bodies, and of the manner in which, in theory, ministers and other public officers are appointed; and the way which Bagehot has so admirably illustrated in his book on the English Constitution, in which the *real* powers of the State, in their relations and oppositions, are described and defined. In the latter way, a description of the German Constitution might be short: there are three estates, it would run, Emperor, Police, and People; but the Emperor is the puppet of the police, and the people's functions are confined to rejecting new laws of a reactionary tendency. As, however, the police are the only interpreters of existing laws, as they constantly interpret these

[1] Bernstein, vol. i. p. 117.

illegally, and silence objections by imprisoning the objectors for disrespect of authority, the power of rejecting new laws is almost nugatory, and the old laws can be made to mean anything.   This description, believe me, is more accurate than any you would find in the bulkiest German tome, *Ueber Verfassungswesen.*

But the above account, though short and simple, is not likely to carry conviction to an English mind ; I will therefore adopt the other, the pedantic method, and describe the written Constitution.

Germany is a federal monarchy ; the King of Prussia is the German Emperor ; and Prussia, by its army, its king and its population, has an immense preponderance in the policy of the Empire.   The Federal Government consists of the following elements : the Emperor and his Minister, the *Reichskanzler,* or Chancellor, form the *first* Estate ; the Chancellor is the only Federal Minister, and is therefore the most important of the Emperor's subjects.   Under Bismarck, and to a less extent under Caprivi, the Chancellor really governed ; the present Chancellor, Fürst zu Hohenlohe, however, is an old man of little force, so that the Emperor is to a great extent his own Chancellor.   The *second* Estate is the *Bundesrath,* which consists of men appointed directly by the kings or princes of the various federated states. In this body, Prussia's influence wholly outweighs that of the other states, and this body is the source from which new bills usually emanate.   Prussia itself has seventeen members out of fifty-eight in this body, but by pressure it is generally able to obtain a majority.   The Prussian Ministers are

members of it, and form a connecting link between
it and the *third* Estate, the *Reichstag*, which is
elected by manhood suffrage of all over the age of
twenty-five. This body has a veto on all new laws,
but new laws are in general proposed, not by it, but
by the Bundesrath. The Reichstag *can* propose a
new law, but in that case, it depends on the consent
of the Chancellor whether its proposal ever comes
up for discussion or not. The Reichstag also has
control of Imperial taxation, but the great bulk of
the taxes are in the hands of the State Governments, which are nowhere democratic. Imperial
taxes consist, in the main, of customs and post-
office; the latter, however, is locally administered
in Bavaria and Würtemberg. The whole of the
Estimates has to be voted by the Reichstag, but a
large part of the sum voted is contributed by the
separate states. Thus, the vast mass of the taxation depends on undemocratic bodies, and the taxes
fall with very undue weight on the necessaries of
the poor. The chief weapon of the Reichstag lies in
refusing supplies for the Army and Navy Estimate;
this Estimate now absorbs about 50 per cent. of
the revenue, and has absorbed, on an average since
1872, about 70 per cent. Owing, however, to the
real and pressing danger of war, and to the ingrained
patriotism of the normal German, refusal of supplies
appears as such an extreme measure that it can
scarcely be resorted to; and whenever the Reichstag
has protested against the immense army expenditure, its dissolution has led to an outburst of
patriotic enthusiasm, and the election of a more
conservative assembly.

It thus appears that great power belongs to the local governments of the Federal states. These are in no sense democratic, but are constituted, usually, in the following manner : The king or prince appoints his Ministers, and also appoints an Upper House. The Lower House is elective, but the vote is always restricted by a property qualification, usually a high one. In Saxony, the only state which has hitherto been fairly democratic, a proposal is now being discussed, and is, apparently, very likely to become law,[1] by which the Prussian system of voting by three classes (*Dreiklassenwahlsystem*) is to be introduced. By this system, which prevails in all Prussian elections, the electors of every district are divided into three classes, according to their fortune : the first class contains a few of the richest men, the second a rather larger number of fairly well-to-do people, the third the mass of the electors —all of whom, however, have to be tax-payers, and are only entitled to vote on producing the tax-collector's receipt. The voting, moreover, is public, and is recorded by officials whose sympathies, naturally, are not on the side of the people. All three classes elect an equal number of men ; in town councils, these men themselves are members, but for the Prussian Diet, where there is a system of double election, as for the American Presidency, these men are only electors. The result of this system of double election is, that the third class, instead of getting one-third of the members, gets none at all : for it elects only one-third of the electors, who are of course outvoted by the other two-thirds.

---

[1] This proposal has now been carried (August 1896).

Not a single Social Democrat sits in the Prussian Diet.

When I add that the Ministers, in fact as in theory, are directly appointed by the Crown, that they are always Conservative, whether they have a majority to back them or not, and that there is thus no connecting link between the popular assembly and the administration, it will be seen that the powers of the people are reduced to a minimum, and that the brief description of the real forces in the State, with which I began, was in no way exaggerated. The danger of war, the army, and the police, make this constitution absolutely rigid and unalterable; there seems no hope of ameliora- tion, as some of the Socialists themselves assert, except from a second Jena—unless, indeed, by a miracle, there should arise an Emperor with some common-sense and common humanity.

It must be remembered also, that trial by jury, the right of coalition, freedom of speech and of the press, exist only in a very limited degree. People accused of political crimes are hardly ever tried by juries; when they are so tried, the State can appeal to a court where there is no jury, as in Lassalle's first trial, in May 1849. Freedom of the press exists, it is true, in so far that anything may be published without previous permission; but the police can always, when it seems good to them, find some pretext for suppressing a newspaper and imprisoning its editors, so that Socialist papers keep a highly-paid responsible *Sitz-Redakteur*, or gaol- editor, who has no real connection with the editorial work, but acknowledges himself to be responsible.

In one respect alone have newspapers perfect freedom, and that is in reporting, without comment, the proceedings of the Reichstag. I had always been told that, in the Reichstag, the members had perfect freedom of speech, and that there did always exist, in this way, one unrestricted outlet for Socialist opinions. To some extent this is true, and especially during the Exceptional Law, Socialist members would often speak for hours, apparently to empty benches, but really, through the press, to their followers and the whole country. But Bebel, on the only occasion when I heard a Social Democrat speak in the Reichstag, was called to order by the President, for mentioning that "in the highest quarters" things had been said against Social Democracy. Some facts about the Emperor, it would appear, are so discreditable, that merely to mention them is an insult to Majesty.

The absence of Democracy appears forcibly to any one on first seeing the Reichstag. The members, like schoolboys, sit below in an amphitheatre, and discuss academic themes; above, on a daïs, sit their schoolmasters, the Chancellor, the Prussian Ministers, and some Prussian officers. Other officers, in full uniform, stand about among the Ministers, and go and come at will. The Tribune has an officer in uniform on each side. From time to time the Ministers, who are members of the Bundesrath, not of the Reichstag, deign to interrupt the academic debate, by communicating the decision at which the Government has arrived on the point in question. The Conservative Benches applaud, and the debate goes on as before. But Party Government, Government by Discussion, control of Parliament over the Ministry—of all this there is not the faintest trace. Officers and Ministry make known their will, and the Reichstag may complain, but can change nothing.

But we must now return to the history of Social Democracy, which we left at the time when the present Constitution was established. People gradually forgot the glories of the war, and the wicked altruism of Social Democracy. The financial crisis of 1873 caused extreme misery in the working classes, and greatly facilitated the spread of socialistic views. The writings of Marx and Lassalle continued to exert an immense influence, and the Socialists carried on more and more vigorously their increasing agitation, by meetings, pamphlets, and newspapers. After 1875 professional agitators were employed, receiving 135 marks (£6, 15s.) a month from the party funds. Their duties consisted in settling in some promising neighbourhood, whence they carried on every kind of agitation. By the time of the Congress of 1876 the party had eight of these full-fledged missionaries, as well as fourteen assistants at lower pay.[1] The union between Lassalleans and Eisenachers at Gotha, in 1875, greatly increased their combined strength. This union was effected by a compromise, in which the positive demands and principles of both parties were acknowledged : thorough - going Collectivism was set forth as the end, and Lassalle's productive associations with State - credit were admitted, under democratic guarantees, as a desirable means. Although this programme showed, on the whole, a victory of the Marxians, Marx protested against

[1] *Nach Zehn Jahren*, vol. i. p. 6.

it in a private letter, as showing only a skin-deep comprehension of his principles. It was felt to be a compromise, and soon ceased to express the opinions of any large section of the party. Owing to the Socialist Law, however, it could not be amended until 1891, in which year it was altered to one which might have satisfied even Marx's imperious demand for orthodoxy.

Meantime, however, Universal Suffrage, which had increased the Socialist vote, had also greatly increased the vote of the Conservatives. The country population of Prussia blindly followed their feudal lords, and many Liberals were terrified into reaction by the advance of Socialism. Thus the Progressive party, which had formerly occupied a mediating position, gradually dwindled, and the two extremes became more and more fiercely antagonistic. Marx's principle of *Klassenkampf*, or class-war, rendered acceptable at first by the cowardly half-heartedness of the Liberals, brought about more and more its own justification, and diminished more and more the parties which might have made a compromise possible The ordinary civil law was enforced with increased stringency, and in the spring of 1878 began the era of chronic *Majestätsbeleidigung* (insult to Majesty), which has continued ever since with varying force. Thus a Socialist history of this period mentions that one man was sentenced at this time to two years and six months' imprisonment because he had hummed to himself in a drunken fit the words, " William is dead; he lives no longer." [1] The bourgeois press urged all employers to refuse work to

[1] *Nach Zehn Jahren*, vol. i. p. 43.

Social Democrats. This measure was also recommended by the Prussian Minister of Commerce in
a circular letter, and many firms declared publicly
that they would henceforth employ no Social Democrats. The reactionary elements, however, were
not yet sufficiently strong to make special legislation against the Socialists possible. The whole
party and all its committees had been declared, in
March 1876, to be dissolved for offences against the
Coalition Law, but it was found that the individual
members could not be "dissolved" under the ordinary law, and exceptional legislation was therefore
demanded. To carry this the Government needed a
fortunate turn of events, which was brought about
by two attempts, in the spring of 1878, on the life of
the Emperor. Though there was not a jot of evidence for Socialist complicity; though, in fact, the two
would-be assassins seem to have been mere muddle-
headed lunatics, the Government and the Conservatives spread a report that these men were Social
Democrats, and a storm of popular indignation broke
out. A repressive measure against Socialism was
laid before the Reichstag after the first attempt, but
was rejected by a considerable majority. Five days
after the second attempt the Chamber was dissolved;
a new one, with fewer Socialists, and many more
Conservatives, was elected; and in October 1878,
the "Exceptional Law against the universally dangerous endeavours of Social Democracy" was hurriedly passed, and instantly came into force. The
provisions of this law, its motives and administration, and the history of Socialism under its rule, will
occupy us in the next lecture.

LECTURE IV

THE EXCEPTIONAL LAW

WE saw, in the last lecture, how the growth of Socialism and the attempts at assassination spread terror through the ranks of the bourgeoisie, and how, by a skilful choice of the moment for dissolution, Bismarck was enabled to obtain a thoroughly reactionary Reichstag. Thus the Exceptional Law was passed, by a majority of 221 to 149, in a Parliament newly elected largely on this issue. It was, therefore, a measure which the Democracy approved of and expressly sanctioned. Apart from the momentary indignation at the attempts on the Emperor's life, the permanent causes of popular enmity to Social Democracy will be worth some discussion, as they still exist, in the main, and are likely long to offer a stubborn resistance to its spread.

The motives for the Law on the part of rulers and capitalists are too obvious to need special comment. When a party proclaims class-warfare as its fundamental principle, it must expect the principle to be taken up by the classes against which its war is directed. But the *popular* enmity which was necessary to the passing of the Law, though in large measure due to the wilful misrepresentation of bourgeois press and bourgeois politicans, was also, and principally, a religious antagonism to the new philosophy of life which Marxianism had introduced. The main aspects of Social Democracy to which this enmity attached itself seem to me to be four: its atheism, its views on marriage and the family, its internationalism, and its advocacy of revolution. In most of these respects, it has suffered greatly from misunderstandings. I shall, therefore, briefly examine its doctrines on these four points.

1. *Atheism.*—At the annual Congress of 1872, a resolution was passed desiring all members of the party to withdraw from religious organisations, and from this time on, the attitude of the party has been avowedly hostile to all existing religions. It is sufficiently evident that the materialistic theory of history leaves no room for religion, since it regards all dogmas as the product of economic conditions. Indeed, Marx's system, as I explained in the first lecture, is itself a complete religion, and cannot, therefore, be tolerant of any other. Just as much as early Christianity, Social Democracy is logically forced to break with all existing faiths, and if it did otherwise, it would lose much of that imposing emotional effect which it derives from its systematic completeness. At the same time, for the purposes of immediate practical politics, this opposition to Christianity must be regarded as a tactical mistake. Lassalle, though himself a sceptic, had not disdained the assistance of the Catholic Church, and had boasted, before the Catholic Rhinelanders, of the support of the Archbishop of Mainz. His successors, however, despised this support—which, it must be confessed, was bought by the sacrifice of perfect

honesty—and they lost, in consequence, the whole of the Rhineland, the former hotbed of the movement, where they are only now beginning, bit by bit, to regain a few seats in the least ultramontane districts. The charge of atheism, in fact, is brought against Social Democracy with the same truth with which it is brought against every new religion—the old dogmas are rejected, and the new ones appear, to those educated in traditional beliefs, to be mere denial and unbelief.

The religion of Social Democracy, however, does lend more colour to the charge of unbelief than most new faiths. For it denies, wholly and unreservedly, any "other world," any spiritual purpose in the universe: it is optimistic, not because it believes that Reason governs the world, but because it is persuaded that the blind forces which control the development of society, whose laws it professes to have discovered, happen to lead, inevitably and unintentionally, to the establishment of a better world—not in some distant heaven, but here on earth, among men and women like ourselves. One of its poets has perfectly expressed this view—

> "Wie schön ist doch die Erde, o wie schön !
> Noch blickt man sehnsuchtsvoll nach Himmelshöhn ;
> Doch hier auf Erden ist das Paradies
> Vom Augenblick, da uns der Fluch verliess—
> Wir wollen bannen diesen Fluch, auf dass
> Zur heil'gen Liebe werde unser Hass." [1]

2. *Views on Marriage and the Family.*—It is universally believed, or at least stated, by opponents

---

[1] Wilhelm Hasenclever, in *Der freie Sänger, Eine Sammlung Sozialdemokratischer Lieder und Deklamationen.* 20th ed. New York, 1893.

of Social Democracy, that it advocates the coarsest forms of free love, that its members are wholly destitute of sexual morality, and that its reign would be the reign of ungoverned licence. As regards the private feelings and characters of its champions, this is so far from being the case, that they are themselves exceptionally moral, and show a distinct aversion to the discussion of all such questions. But as regards their theoretic doctrines, the ordinary view is true to this extent, that they believe the form of the family, like every other social institution, to be dependent on economic causes, and regard it as a changing form, consequently, which cannot subsist unaltered in the Collectivist State. The best and most condensed expression of their views on this point, as on almost every other, is to be found in the Communist Manifesto.

Abolition of the family! Even the most Radical grow hot over this shameful intention of the Communists.

On what does the present bourgeois family rest? On capital, on private gain. It exists in its complete development only for the bourgeoisie; but it finds its complement in the proletariats' forced want of family life, and in public prostitution.

The family of the bourgeois naturally disappears with the disappearance of this, its complement, and both disappear with the vanishing of capital.

Do you cast it up against us that we wish to abolish the exploitation of children by their parents? We admit this crime.

But, you say, we destroy the most intimate relations, by substituting, for education by parents, education by society.

And is not your education also determined by society? By the social relations within which you educate, by the more or less direct action of society through the school, &c. ? The Communists have not invented the influence of society on education; they only alter its character, they rescue education from the influence of the ruling class.

The bourgeois ways of speaking about the family and education, about the sacred relation of parents and children, grow the more sickening, the more, in consequence of the progress of industry, all family bonds are torn asunder for the proletariat, and children are transformed into articles of commerce and instruments of labour.

"But you Communists wish to introduce community of women," the whole bourgeosie shrieks in chorus against us.

The bourgeois sees in his wife a mere instrument of production. He hears that instruments of production are to be exploited in common, and naturally cannot imagine but that women will share the same fate.

He does not guess that this is the very problem, to abolish the position of women as mere instruments of production.

Moreover, nothing is more laughable than the highly moral horror of our bourgeois about the Communists' supposed official community of women. Communists do not need to introduce community of women; it has almost always existed. . . .

It is self-evident that with the abolition of the present conditions of production would disappear also the consequent community of women, *i.e.*, official and unofficial prostitution.

From this passage, as from all the writings of Social Democrats on the subject, their real attitude is clear. They wish, by securing the economic independence of women, as of labourers, to change marriage from a money purchase of legal property into a free choice on both sides, dictated not by economic motives, but by feeling. Existing strict monogamy,

they say, rests, like prostitution, on the economic
slavery of women, and the Communist state would
enable a woman, when strong and adequate grounds
existed, to leave her husband without losing her
only means of livelihood. They would, perhaps,
object to all *legal* restrictions, but they would
most certainly not approve of unbridled licence,
which they regard—certainly with some justice—as
facilitated much more by the present possibility of
purchase, than by a state of society where free choice
alone would rule.[1]

3. *Internationalism.*—In Germany, which has but
lately emerged, by a series of successful but arduous
wars, from a state of division and political unim-
portance, the self-preservative instinct of aggressive
patriotism has a force which no English Jingo could
approach. Positive enmity to France, as the means
by which national unity and power were achieved,
seems to all ranks of society a solemn duty. In
such a milieu, the idea of internationalism, which
with us is a mere commonplace, appears as a monstrous and immoral paradox, and can only be understood as positive friendliness to the enemy. Even
to the educated and cultivated German, it seems quite
out of the question that all the real interests of the
nation, so far as they are not bought by the dis-
grace and lasting enmity of others, can be equally
dear to a party which does not regard murder of
Frenchmen as the most sacred of duties. " They
mock at the holiest feelings of the nation," people
say, and no amount of reiterated explanation can
make clear to these people the very simple notion

[1] For a fuller treatment of this subject, see Appendix.

that one country has no greater claim to happiness or prosperity than another. This is almost the strongest of all the objections to Social Democracy, and has hindered its growth more, perhaps, than any other single cause.

4. *Advocacy of Revolution.*—The position of Social Democracy on the question of Revolution, which has been adopted by its friends and misunderstood by its enemies with remarkable consistency, is sufficiently explained by the passage which I quoted from Liebknecht in my last lecture. Social Democrats invariably use the word Revolution, in accordance with the dialectical theory of development by sudden transitions, to mean, not a forcible resistance to established authority, but any great organic change in the constitution of society. In this sense Lassalle declared, as we saw, that Arkwright's cotton-spinning machine was a revolution ; in this sense he declared, when defending himself in Court against the charge of revolution-making, " It (the Revolution) will either come in full legality, with all the blessings of peace, if people have the wisdom to resolve, in time and from above, on its introduction, or it will break in, within a certain time, under all the convulsions of force, with wildly-waving locks and iron sandals on its feet." As regards the latter alternative, Revolution, in the ordinary sense of the word, Social Democrats hold, like every serious political party, that they will be justified, at any time when they may attain supreme power, in introducing the changes they desire by any means which may be necessary. They hold, with Lassalle, that in questions of constitution, might alone is right, and

that, when they have won the might, any surviving opposition may be rightfully suppressed. But they distinguish between *might* (*Macht*) and *force* (*Gewalt*): the latter, they say, is usually a reactionary power, and is embodied in the army and the police. To use force without being backed by real might, is the policy of the Anarchists, which is uniformly condemned by all responsible Social Democrats.[1] But the development of society leads necessarily, so they say, to a continual increase in the number of wage-earners, and a continual diminution in the number of capitalists. We have only to agitate, therefore, to make wage-earners aware of their class-interests, and in time we are sure of winning the preponderant *might*. Whether, when that stage is reached, we are compelled to use *force*, must depend entirely on our opponents. But till that time the use of force would be folly, since it could not fail to lead to defeat.

It is important to be clear on this point, as Social Democrats are persistently regarded by their opponents as a set of vulgar revolutionaries, prepared at any moment, wantonly and for the fun of the thing, to cut their neighbours' throats and cause a temporary reign of terror. In reality, no other attitude than theirs seems possible to serious people; to have the power and not use it, would be cowardice and treachery to the cause.[2]

[1] *Vide* Liebknecht's speech on this subject at the Sanct-Gallen Congress, 1887.

[2] To prove the correctness of the above account, I subjoin a list of references: Marx, " Capital," English translation, vol. i. p. 776 ; Lassalle, *Reden und Schriften*, ed. Bernstein, vol. ii. pp. 22, 23, 24, 383 ; *Der Hochverraths-Prozess wider Liebknecht, Bebel und Hepner,*

The above four main causes of popular hatred, together with the momentary panic from the attempts on the Emperor's life, sufficiently account for the election of a thoroughly reactionary Parliament. The measure which was laid by Bismarck before the new Reichstag, against the "universally dangerous endeavours of Social Democracy," though originally designed to expire in May 1881, was prolonged by successive Parliaments, without essential alteration, until October 1890.   Its most important provisions were the following :—

§ 1. Associations which aim, by Social Democratic, Socialistic, or Communistic endeavours, at the destruction of the existing order in State or society, are to be forbidden.

The same holds of Associations in which such endeavours make their appearance in a manner dangerous to the peace, or, in particular, to the harmony between different classes of the population.

§ 9. Meetings in which Social Democratic, Socialistic, or Communistic tendencies, directed to the destruction of the existing order in State or society, make their appearance, are to be dissolved.

Meetings, of which facts justify the assumption that they are destined to further such tendencies, are to be forbidden.

Public festivities and processions are placed under the same restrictions.

§ 11. Printed matter, in which Social Democratic,

Berlin, 1895, pp. 71, 160–161 ; Bebel, *Unsere Ziele,* 10th ed., pp. 19, 53 ; *Protokoll des Wydener Kongresses der deutschen Sozialdemokratic,* Zurich, 1880, p. 40 ; *Sanct-Gallen Protokoll,* Hottingen-Zurich, 1888, pp. 39–43 ; *Nach Zehn Jahren,* London, 1889, vol. i. pp. 55, 67, 70–71, 80.

Socialistic, or Communistic tendencies, directed to the destruction of the existing order in State and society in a manner dangerous to the peace and, in particular, to the harmony between different classes of the population, make their appearance, is to be forbidden.

In the case of periodical literature, the prohibition can be extended to any further issue, as soon as a single number has been forbidden under this law.

§ 16. The collection of contributions for the furthering of Social Democratic, Socialistic, or Communistic endeavours, directed toward the destruction of the existing order in State or society, as also the public instigation to the furnishing of such contributions, are to be forbidden by the police.

§ 20. . . . The money obtained (by the police) from forbidden collections, or the value of the same, is to be declared to have fallen to the poor-relief fund of the neighbourhood.

§ 24. Persons who make a business of furthering the above-described endeavours, or who have been legally punished under this law, can be deprived by the police of the right to spread literature publicly, either in the course of business or otherwise, as also of the right to the itinerant sale of literature.

§ 28. For districts or localities which are threatened, by the above-mentioned endeavours, with danger to the public safety, the following provisions can be made, for the space of a year at most, by the central police of the state in question, and subject to the permission of the Bundesrath.

(1) That meetings may only take place with the previous permission of the police; this prohibition does not extend to meetings for an election to the Reichstag or the Diet.

(2) That the distribution of printed matter may not take place in public roads, streets, or places, or other public localities.

(3) That residence in such districts or localities can be forbidden to all persons from whom danger to the public safety or order is to be feared.

(4) That the possession, import, or sale of weapons is forbidden, limited, or confined by certain conditions.

The places where this last paragraph was applied were said to be in a minor state of siege. For all the other paragraphs, the local police were the administrators. The usual punishment consisted of a fine of 500 marks (£25), or three months' imprisonment, for the less responsible followers; with longer terms of imprisonment for the leaders.

But it is not from the nominal text of this law that its real nature can be learnt. As I pointed out in discussing the Constitution, the absence of a connecting link between the Reichstag and the executive enables the police to administer the law illegally, and in the present instance, they made the fullest use of this power.

The leaders of the Social Democratic party had resolved that the wisest policy was to wait quietly to see how the law would be administered. In all the later numbers of the official organ, *Vorwärts* readers were warned that the Government wished to drive them to desperation, that rash deeds of violent resistance would only be of service to the reaction, and that it was important above all to avoid every unnecessary illegality. For weeks, every number contained, in large print, this warning:—

"Comrades in the work! Do not allow yourselves to be provoked! They wish to fire! The reaction needs riots to win the game."

Then, in the number published on the day when the act came into force, it warned its readers that henceforth it must moderate its tone, must grow colourless and flat, but that it might be trusted to keep the same views at heart.

But although *Vorwärts* and all the other party papers, to the number of fifty, adopted this milder tone, and carefully avoided all controversial matter —except dry facts, which, under a despotic Government, are apt to become controversial—the police were not to be outwitted. They judged by the former tendency of these papers, and suppressed *Vorwärts* and the two next most important journals in the first week. By the end of a month, there existed, in the whole of Germany, two alone of the fifty Socialist papers; and these two only survived by adroitly changing their name and tone *before* the law came into force. In this way, almost all the Social Democratic journalists were deprived of their only means of subsistence. All Socialistic organisations, except the electoral associations, were quickly dissolved; even these, at first, were allowed no activity. Under these rapid blows, the party naturally lost its unity; its central government— vested of necessity in the members of the Reichstag, as the only association which could not be dissolved —was unable to establish any close relations with the scattered disorganised members, and became unpopular with some by its ardent and reiterated exhortations to order and patience. But scarcely were the press and the organisation effectually destroyed than the Government proceeded, on November 28th, only a month after the law had come into force, in spite of the almost death-like legality of the Social Democrats, to proclaim the minor state of siege over Berlin. Sixty-seven Social Democrats were banished from Berlin on the first day. These exiles issued together the first Socialist leaflet illegally published under the Exceptional Law, a very typical, instructive document, of which the following is a free translation :—

To our friends and comrades in Berlin.

We, the undersigned, having been stigmatised by the authority of the police as persons from whom a " danger to public order and safety is to be feared," have been banished from Berlin and its neighbourhood.

Before we give effect to this decision, and before we desert our homes and our families to go into banishment, we hold it our duty to address a few words to you, our comrades.

People cast it up against us that we endanger public order.

Comrades and friends ! You know that as long as we were among you, and could speak to you by voice and pen, our first and last word was :

No deeds of violence; observe the laws, but fight for your rights within the laws !

We wish as our farewell to you to repeat these words for the last time, and to urge you to observe them now more than ever, let the future bring what it may.

Do not allow yourselves to be provoked !

Do not forget that an infamous system of newspaper lies has succeeded in representing us to public opinion as men capable of every disgraceful act, as men whose purpose is destruction and deeds of violence.

Every mistake of a single one among us would have the worst consequences for us all, and would give the reaction a justification for its coercive measures.

Comrades! Working-men of Berlin! We go from your midst into exile; as yet we do not know how far the fury of persecution may drive us, but be assured of this: wherever we may tarry, we shall always remain faithful to the common cause, we shall always hold aloft the banner of the proletariat. But to you our request is, *keep the peace!* Let our enemies rage and slander us, heed them not!

Repel the tempters who wish to incite you to riots or secret combinations!

Hold fast to the solution which we have so often proclaimed to you: By our legality our enemies will be brought to destruction!

And now, one last word, Friends and Comrades! The decree of banishment has hitherto fallen, with one exception, only on the fathers of families.

Not one of us is able to leave to those dependent on him, more than the support of the next few days.

Comrades! *remember our wives and our children.*

Fellow-workers, keep the peace! Long live the Proletariat! Long live Social Democracy!

With Social Democratic greetings:

[Here the signatures of the exiled.]

This leaflet was naturally confiscated, nevertheless it was distributed by thousands throughout Berlin.

The minor state of siege was afterwards proclaimed in several other big towns, in Hamburg, Leipzig, Frankfort on the Main, and other places; in all of these, the next elections showed a great increase in the Socialist vote, although the aggregate vote of the party throughout the country considerably decreased. The first rapid blows of the per-

secution destroyed all confidence, all feeling of
organised unity, in the party, and at the Congress
of Schloss-Wyden, in 1880, the general tone was
one of great though resolute depression. This Congress, which, like those of 1883 and 1887, was held
in the utmost secrecy, took place in a remote district of Switzerland, in an old ruined castle, which
had been quietly fitted up with dormitories and
beds of straw for the occasion. A neighbouring
town was secretly indicated to the delegates as the
place of meeting, but when they arrived, a local
Socialist referred them, one by one, to the castle
where the Congress really took place. Thus the
vigilance of Government was eluded, and many
delegates were able to return without having been
discovered. The official report, which was published in Zurich, mentions none of the names of the
speakers, and reports the speeches very briefly.

In some respects, the outlook was already a better
one than under the first shock of the Exceptional
Law. The suppression of the German press had
led, in the first place, to the establishment of an
extreme revolutionary paper in London, *Die Frei-
heit*, and then, in the autumn of 1879, to the
foundation of a new official organ in Zurich, the
Sozialdemokrat. This paper, which was secretly distributed with the greatest energy, and soon began
to make a large profit for the party funds, restored,
in some measure, the connection between the central
authority and the individual members. In all the
three Congresses held under the Socialist Law, however, the chief difficulty arose from the unruly
violence of the extreme party, who advocated the

so-called "Propaganda of Action," and objected to
the moderate attitude of the leaders. Although,
in the passage of the programme which declared
that the party would strive, by all *legal* means, for
a free state and a socialistic society, the word *legal*
was unanimously struck out by the Congress of
1880, there were many, especially among refugees
in foreign countries, who were still dissatisfied, who
thought—or declared, to cover past cowardice—that
forcible revolt was the only proper course, that the
members of the Reichstag had become traitors, and
that the policy of passive resistance was cowardly
and dishonest. The most extreme supporters of
this view split off and formed an Anarchist party
of their own, which, however, remained small and
unimportant. The less extreme advocates of revolution contented themselves with opposition to the
leaders, whose policy was rendered very difficult
by Bismarck's measures of "social reform." These
measures, which provided insurance against accident,
sickness, and old age, were, so far as they went,
socialistic. It was Bismarck's aim, first to muzzle
the official Social Democrats, and then, by a series
of small bribes, to wean the proletariat from their
adherence to revolutionary principles. Bismarck's
State Socialism has excited the admiration of many
critics, and it is often supposed that Socialists have
been ungrateful in not supporting it more cordially.
But in reality the name is very misleading, for
there is much more State than Socialism in his
policy. This policy may be briefly described as
military and bureaucratic despotism, tempered by
almsgiving. Leaving aside the large parts of his

so-called Socialistic legislation which were purely re-actionary and mediæval—re-establishment of guilds, protective duties, &c.—the measures of Progressive Socialism turn out, on inspection, to be designed rather for ornament than for use. The principle of Bismarck's Insurance Laws is, roughly, that employer and employed, in every branch of wage-earning labour, shall each contribute a small weekly premium, in return for which the workman receives, in the event of accident, sickness, or old age, and those dependent on him receive in case of his death, a weekly payment, whose amount depends on the previous premium paid by the workman in question. This is excellent in theory, but in practice, the expenses of weekly collection are heavy, and the extension of bureaucracy is vexatious, while no benefit is received from the old age insurance till the age of seventy, and then the sum received can-not exceed 191 marks (about £9, 10s.) a year, and may not exceed 106.40 marks (about £5, 6s.) a year. Thus the real gain to the labourer is very minute. Nevertheless, the principle of Bismarck's Insurance Laws was one which Socialists could not but approve; the Social Democratic members, there-fore, in general supported them, but the majority of the active party, more impressed by the motive than by the effect of these laws, were inclined to regard any support of Bismarck as treachery. Thus a division arose between the members of the Reichs-tag—who by law were the only possible central authority—and the majority of the party which lasted till the expiration of the Socialist Law in 1890. This division, as well as the attempt to recon-

struct an organisation, afforded great material to the
police, and one worthy member of this maligned
body, in a gem of police logic and psychology, entitled "The Secret Organisation of Social Democracy," [1] throws much light on its difficulties at
this time, as also, though unintentionally, on the
spirit in which the Exceptional Law was administered. Lest it should seem that we have regarded matters too exclusively from the Socialist
standpoint, let us look, for a moment, through the
spectacles of this energetic saviour of society, whose
profound knowledge of human nature is only sur-
passed by the imaginative wealth of his metaphors.
He begins, "The battle for the binding of the hydra
of Socialism seemed, for a time, more or less hope-
less, despite the Exceptional Law, but this is a
perspective which has now, fortunately, completely
disappeared. We have three factors to thank
chiefly for this result : in the first place, the unin-
terrupted and unwearying watchfulness of our *police
force*, which opposes without scruple every breach
and overstepping of the law on the part of Social
Democracy. The second factor is the German
magistracy, one of whose noblest duties lies in un-
masking the dark sneaking courses of those whose
sole purpose is the undermining of our present
society ; and thirdly, it depends on the unanimous
co-operation of all *loyal elements*, in opposing, with
determination and insight, the public, as well as
secret, agitation of the Socialist leaders. If these
three factors can preserve our present position, then
it becomes a fact that Socialism *has attained its*

[1] 2nd edition, 1887.

highest point! But the moment the smallest concession is made to this party, if only tacitly, or by
remissness in punishments, the results we have won
are made doubtful!"

Our friend now proceeds to the Exceptional Law
and its direct consequences.

The Progressives, he regrets to say, have begun,
by arguments unworthy of an answer, to oppose this
law, because they desire Socialist votes in the second
ballots.

When the Socialist law was first passed, the party
was almost annihilated. The officials, of course,
were first hit. Some of these gentlemen changed
their views, others left Germany, either soon to forget their Socialistic lusts in voluntary exile, or to
carry on, from England or America, an Anarchist
war " for the liberation of their German brothers."
The final remnant of the agitators who could not, or
would not, abandon the occupation they had grown
fond of—observe the subtle psychology of this point
—sought to accommodate themselves to the altered
circumstances of the Exceptional Law, by endeavour-
ing to display in their doings a very noticeable
moderation. . . . The working - men themselves,
against whom, least of all, the law was directed, were
liberated by it from a party dictation which, with
its costly apparatus of agitation and officials, demanded the highest sacrifices of money and time.
Hence the law had, for the first two or three years,
all the desired consequences.

The change in the circumstances of the party,
between 1881 and 1885, was rendered possible, he
explains, by its attempting an organisation against

which, in its opinion, the Exceptional Law could raise no objection. The Government, it is true, instantly saw through these tactics, and the breaches were perceived to which, in this proceeding, the Exceptional Law could point. But the general Criminal Law gave of itself an instrument for invalidating this attempted organisation. The action in Elberfeldt, it is true, against the participators in the Wyden Congress broke down, because the organisation, then just beginning, did not yet offer sufficient material for a judicial sentence.[1]

After a partially correct account of their organisation, our friend comes to the growth of Social Democracy since the elections of 1881. By means of this new organisation, he says, Social Democracy has again been enabled to grow to an alarming extent. Moreover, the law is not uniformly administered in the different states, and in some they are actually allowed to publish a few newspapers. The Trade Unions—which in Germany are by law forbidden to touch politics—have also been exploited for agitation ; the leaders, however, wisely

---

[1] He refers here to the prosecutions for secret conspiracy, which were brought, after all three Congresses, against those of the participators whom the Government could lay hands on. At first these prosecutions failed, but after an acquittal of the participators in the Copenhagen Congress (1883), the Government, determined to have its way, declared the verdict invalid, and ordered a second trial. In this trial it was decided that the official leaders of the party, since the forbidden *Sozialdemokrat* was their official organ, and they incited their followers to distribute it, constituted an association for incitement to illegal actions. They were all sentenced to six months' imprisonment ; the *Sozialdemokrat* publicly declared that, since it had brought punishment on the leaders by being the official organ, it was no longer the official organ but would preserve its former tone, and all went on as before.

remain in the background, and utilise a race of younger men whom they have enveloped in their toils. He then sets forth with great care the illegality of the organisation, but he naïvely remarks that convictions can only be obtained with great difficulty, for the secret organisation of Social Democracy " is undeniably a sly and careful piece of work." Hence it is not surprising if a Court does not at once perceive the necessity of an unfavourable verdict.

He concludes with a description of the radical and moderate sections of the party. The moderation of the moderate section he regards, true to the traditions of his calling, as wholly the result of the Socialist law. The radical section, he says, is kept alive by the *Sozialdemokrat*, for which he reserves some of his choicest language. After describing the " cynical mockeries and vulgar revilings of all that is holy to every nationally-minded German," he proceeds : " The coarse jokes and vulgar obscenities which are sprinkled throughout its contents are well calculated to enchain the unjudging mass of readers, who then absorb the contents with greedy haste." This wicked paper, and the centralised organisation, that high school of revolution, keep alive the revolutionary spirit. Let the police be given powers to fight these more vigorously, and the hydra will become a perspective which has vanished. This Cheshire cat consummation, we must all agree, is worthy the best energies of every true-hearted German.

The above account of the reorganisation and revival of the party, in spite of the source from which it flows, appears to be substantially correct. It is impossible to discover the exact nature of the Socialist organisation under the Exceptional Law, as the Social Democrats naturally published no accounts of it, and are reticent, for fear of future persecutions, of giving any information on the subject. It is certain, however, that trade unions, singing clubs, clubs for workmen's education, and all manner of innocent-sounding bodies, were freely used for Socialist propaganda. Committees for the local agitation, which were always small, so as not to attract attention, used to meet " to celebrate a friend's birthday," to go for a Sunday walk in the country, or for some other harmless purpose. In all important centres there was, as at present, a confidential agent (*Vertrauensmann*), whose business it was to distribute the *Sozialdemokrat* and other forbidden literature, or to indicate addresses to which packages of contraband literature could be sent from abroad. The confidential agent also had to collect money for general party purposes, and especially for the support of those whom persecution had deprived of the means of subsistence. In this respect, the Social Democrats showed, from the first, the most amazing spirit and self-sacrifice. Although almost all of them belonged to the poorest classes, and although collections of money for party purposes were heavily punished by the law, they yet succeeded in supporting the wives and families of all who had been imprisoned or banished, and in subscribing compensation for those who had been fined. At first, candidates for the Reichstag had not been allowed to publish even election addresses or leaflets, but after 1881 the Government, finding that the Socialists, in spite of all its efforts, had obtained twelve members in the place of nine, adopted a milder administration of the law. Bismarck still hoped, by this mildness and by his "Social Reform," to tempt the working-men from the paths of Socialism; but after two elections, those of 1884 and 1887, had shown an increase of unparalleled rapidity in the Socialist vote, the law was again administered with nearly the old rigour. Gradually, however, by the continued increase of the party, everybody except Bismarck became convinced of its uselessness; with the accession of the present Emperor, who wished to pose, like Frederick the Great, as the king of beggars, a more friendly attitude was adopted towards the working classes. Bismarck was dismissed, and the Law was allowed, after a last fruitless attempt at renewal in a milder form, to expire on September 30, 1890.[1]

Under this infamous Law, the crowning endeavour of the enlightened police state, an aggregate punishment of 831 years' imprisonment—to say nothing of fines, banishments, &c.—was inflicted on the Social Democrats of Germany. It is by this Law that Bismarck is remembered among them, and if they seem ungrateful for his Positive Reform and State-Socialism, we must remember what the German State is—we must remember that State-Socialism means an increase of the powers of Absolutism and

---

[1] The defeat, in the spring of 1895, of the *Umsturzvorlage*, a less strenuous proposal for repressive legislation, gives grounds for the hope that future bills of a similar tendency will not be carried, and that Exceptional Laws are at an end.

Police Rule, and that acquiescence in such a state, whatever bribes it may offer to labour, is acquiescence in the suppression of all free speech and all free thought; is acquiescence in intellectual stagnation and moral servility.

LECTURE V

WITH the expiration of the Socialist Law, three
main questions arose out of the altered circumstances
of the party, that of their future tactics, of the reform of their programme, and of the organisation to
be adopted in future. The first two of their Party
Congresses, which could now be held in Germany
in all publicity, were almost wholly concerned with
these three points. The first Congress, that of
Halle, met twelve days after the expiration of the
law, in a festively-decorated hall containing the
image of Freedom, and portraits of Marx and Lassalle over the tribune, and pictures, surrounded with
garlands, of the leaders who had died in the meantime. Here the delegates congratulated each other
on their deliverance, and here they set to work to
build up afresh, on a larger scale than before, the
organisation which the persecution had shattered.

I. *Organisation.*—The new organisation was a
masterpiece of ingenuity and efficiency. The task
of organising is, in Germany, a very different task
from any that could be imagined in England. For
the question to be solved is not, what organisation

will be most effectual ? but, what organisation will
evade the Coalition Laws of the different states ?
This evasion is the determining motive of the whole
system, and the Coalition Laws must be understood
before its *raison d'être* can be grasped.

Of the wanton severity of these iniquitous laws it
is difficult for Englishmen, except by watching their
actual operation, to form any conception. Most of
them were passed in or about 1850, the year of
reaction, but successive interpretations, by a gene-
ration of servile legal ingenuity, have rendered their
present meaning far more galling than that borne by
their obvious interpretation. They differ in every
state, but in the three most important states,
Prussia, Saxony, and Bavaria, they are fairly similar.
I will take the Prussian law—which is very far from
being the worst—as my text, and indicate important
differences in other states as occasion arises.

The Prussian law is designed, as its title in-
forms us, to prevent the misuse, dangerous to legal
freedom (*sic*) and order, of the right of meeting
and combination. By its provisions, any society
which is designed to consider public affairs is subject to the following restrictions. Its existence,
its rules, and the description of its members must
be notified to the police, within three days of its
foundation, by its officers or other management ;
any subsequent change of rules must be similarly
notified. Societies whose existence, purpose, or
constitution is secret, which demand obedience to
unknown persons, or unconditional obedience to any
one, are illegal, and all their members are punishable. Servants, sailors, and agricultural labourers

are forbidden to combine for the purpose of influencing their employers in any way. This restriction used to apply also to miners and artisans; but among these, Trade Unions are now tolerated by the law. In some states there is an elastic paragraph, forbidding societies which have any " immoral purpose." As an illustration of the interpretation of this clause, I may instance a case which occurred in Saxony. A union, which had a rule that its members should not work overtime, expelled a member who transgressed this rule. This was regarded as an immoral interference with personal liberty (!) and the union was dissolved. State employees, including those in railways and State mines, must not belong to any society systematically opposed to the Government.

Any non-political association, *e.g.*, a Trade Union, can be, and is dissolved, if it touches on public affairs, and the police may examine even the statutes of non-political associations.

Political associations which call meetings must not (1) " contain or allow in their meetings any women, scholars, or apprentices; " or (2) "enter into connection with other associations, even if these be non-political, for any common purpose, whether by letters, committees, central organs or officers, or in any other way."

The second of these restrictions exists in almost all the states; the first, which applies also to political associations of women, or students only, exists in Prussia, Bavaria, Brunswick, and some smaller states. It prevents the presence of women, scholars, and apprentices, even in non-political meetings, such as balls or social evenings.

As regards the definition of an association (*Verein*), it is constituted by any voluntary union of several people, for a common purpose under a common management. Three people have, in some cases, been regarded as a sufficient number. If the other qualities of an association exist, without the management, the law is not evaded, but punishes the members for having no management. Commissions or committees, if they have any durable functions, count as associations.[1]

An association need never have met, need not have any particular number of members, and membership does not presuppose a knowledge of its purposes. If an association extends over more than one police-district—a case regarded by the law as abnormal—notice of its constitution must be given to the police of each district. If the members of one district have any independent activity, even a meeting, they form a branch-association, which has to give separate notice, and a connection between two such branches is interpreted as illegal, under the above provisions. We have next to consider the definition of politics or public affairs, which is equally liberal. These include communal, ecclesiastical, and religious affairs, as also social questions of any wide scope. Thus, for example, a trade union becomes political, as soon as it considers the conditions

---

[1] I may mention, as an instance of the legal definition of an association, that in November 1895, while I was in Germany, a business meeting of the staff of a Social Democratic newspaper, the *Magdcburg Volkstimme*, was dissolved by seven policemen, for not having given due notice to the police, on the ground that it was a meeting of a political association, in which public affairs were being discussed. Vide *Vorwärts*, November 23, 1895.

which determine wages in general, or even the wages
of its own trade as a whole.   In Saxony, all trade
unions are regarded as political, and are therefore
subject to the restrictions imposed on political associations.

So much for the right of association; the right
of meeting, which is declared by the Prussian Constitution to be permitted to all Prussians without
police permission, must be next considered.   As
regards the definition of a meeting, it is simple:
anything is a meeting which assembles, at a particular place and time, for any common purpose.   It
need not have a chairman, it need not have been
previously called, it need not consist of any particular
number of people; it need not even, as I was told by
a waggish lawyer, be aware that it is a meeting.
Nevertheless, if it *is* a meeting, but has no chairman, it is punishable.   If a meeting is to discuss
public affairs, forty-eight hours' notice must be given
to the police, and one or two representatives of the
police must be present, to give an official report of
the proceedings to the authorities.   In Saxony, a
meeting may be forbidden if danger to public order
is to be feared from it, and the police, in this respect,
show themselves remarkably timorous.

A meeting may not pass any resolution under a
collective name, nor may a collection of money be
proposed, while the meeting is taking place.   Open-
air meetings and processions are forbidden altogether
in some states; in the rest, including Prussia, they
require forty-eight hours' notice, and may be forbidden without assigned reason.   Anything in the
open air is a procession, if it attracts general atten-

tion. Moreover, invitations to an open-air meeting cannot be given, until permission to hold it has been obtained, and, as the police need not give permission within any stated time, the right to meet can thus be rendered nugatory.

It must be borne in mind that the Coalition Laws, though transgressed with impunity by every other party, are always interpreted, where Social Democracy is concerned, with the utmost severity of which they are susceptible; thus, Prussian trade unions, whose members are almost all Social Democrats, cannot in any way take part in the political agitation, and therefore lose half the vigour and interest which characterise trade unions in England.

The only important exceptions to the law are the members of any party in the Reichstag, and the local electoral associations, designed solely to influence the elections in a particular constituency. But even these latter become illegal as soon as they combine with any other political organisation.

Under these circumstances, it will be seen that the formation of a legal organisation, extending over the whole country, and having branches in separate localities, is a problem of great difficulty, whose solution requires no ordinary ingenuity. At the discussion of the Party Congress in 1890, many were for giving up the attempt, and most proposals had to be rejected as illegal. A solution was, however, finally arrived at, which has hitherto succeeded in outwitting the crown jurists.

The party has no fixed membership, but acknowledges as a *Genosse*, or comrade, every one who agrees with the programme, and supports the party according to his powers. The members, thus loosely defined, do not constitute an association, and can therefore choose, in the separate parliamentary constituencies, delegates to the *Parteitag*, or Annual Congress. No constituency may choose more than three delegates, but otherwise there is no restriction as to number or sex, it being understood, that only those places where Social Democracy is strong will send more than one delegate. If no women are chosen in this way, they may be chosen by separate women's meetings. The Annual Congress further contains the Socialist members of the Reichstag, and the members of the party executive (*Parteileitung*). The latter formed the permanent central government of the party, and were chosen by the Congress. It consisted of two presidents, two secretaries, a treasurer, and seven members of committee. The presidents were paid 50 marks (£2, 10s.) a month each, the secretaries and treasurer 150 marks (£7, 10s.) each; they had to reside in Berlin, and were expected to live chiefly by their private earnings. This central government had no recognised connection with the local organisations, which, to gain the benefit of the law, consist of electoral associations in the separate constituencies. These contain only the more active local members of the party, and have a president, secretary, and treasurer of their own. But besides these officers, there exists a *Vertrauensperson*, or confidential agent, chosen, not by the electoral association, but by a public meeting, called by a private member of the party, and open, theoretically, to members of every political party.

Practically, however, good care is taken that only *Genossen* are present, and the man or woman chosen becomes the most important of the local members. But as he has no official connection with any organisation whatever, he is able to carry on correspondence with the central Party Government, and so to form the connecting link between the localities and the Central Executive. It is his duty to collect money for the party, to distribute literature—especially forbidden literature and agitation-leaflets—and to communicate the wishes of the Central Government to his locality. The method of collecting money—on which subject the law has many vexatious regulations—is as simple as it is excellent. The Party prints large numbers of *bons*, as they are called; they look like postage stamps, and have printed on them S. P. D., 10 pf. These are issued to the various confidential agents, who distribute them among trustworthy persons. The latter then dispose of them by ones and twos at meetings, in ordinary talk, or at any convenient opportunity, at the rate of 10 pf. for each. Thus small sums can be easily collected, and the number of *bons* sold is an automatic record of the receipts, which saves the complicated accounts otherwise necessary for such small sums. The collectors give all the money they have obtained to the confidential agent of their locality, and he pays it into the Party funds. In case of fraudulence on the part of the collectors, the confidential agent has of course no legal remedy, but is compelled to make up the missing sum out of his own pocket. Thus all depends on the self-sacrifice, honesty, and diligence of the individual members, and in this respect, I believe, their public spirit leaves little to be desired.[1]

In the distribution of literature and leaflets, also, the confidential agent's personal knowledge of the members is of supreme importance. So efficient is the organisation in this respect, that the Socialists boast of being able to flood all Berlin with agitation leaflets in two hours. This is not so easy a task as in London, for distribution of leaflets, announcements of meetings, &c., are only allowed in private rooms; they must be given separately to all the inhabitants of a house divided into flats, and may not be left with the hall porter or distributed in the hall, nor must they be distributed in shops, or other places to which the public have access. In country districts, where there are fewer members, the machine is, of course, much more imperfect; it is still a question here of pioneer agitation by public meetings, and private propaganda by special emissaries. But wherever there are enough members to form the framework of an organisation, there the organisation is sure to be excellent.

I have still to mention one essential point. The organisation of the party, as we have seen, is legal, but the administration of the law is illegal. Conse-

---

[1] The efficiency of this system may be gathered from the Party's accounts, which are published monthly and discussed at the Annual Congress. Thus, in the eleven months, from 1st October 1894 to 31st August 1895, the five Berlin divisions represented by Social Democrats contributed to current expenses—exclusive of defence of accused persons and other extras—sums making a total of about 36,000 marks, or nearly 40,000 marks annually. Election expenses are paid by a special collection. The total income of the Party chest amounts to about 250,000 marks, or £12,500 annually.

quently, on the 29th of November 1895, the Party Government, the Press Committee, and the six Berlin electoral associations were dissolved by the police. This occurred as the result of a simultaneous raid on the houses of eighty leading Social Democrats, in which the police searched through all the cupboards, under the beds, and even in the ash-bins; illegally confiscated all the *bons* and every scrap of paper they could find, written and printed. Their excuse for closing the above organisations lay in regarding the Berlin Confidential Agents as an association; which they explicitly and definitely are not. The Social Democrats, more used to these methods than I, had never hoped to form an organisation which would stand permanently. After the raid, I met one of the leaders of the party, and asked if the police could find any ground for dissolving the organisation. "The police can do everything," he replied; "merely to ask such a question is a libel on the Government." And this proved to be the truth.[1]

On the occasion of this decision the *Vossische Zeitung* (December 1st), the most respectable of bourgeois papers, the *Times* of Germany, remarked :—

"If the closing of the associations is confirmed, the whole Social Democratic organisation will be destroyed thereby. It is remarkable that it has taken the police more than five years to recognise the illegality of the Social Democratic organisation. This organisation was proposed, in all publicity, at the first party Congress after the fall of the Socialist Law, which took place at Halle in October 1890.

---

[1] The legal proceedings have now confirmed the action of the police, but are said to have persuaded public opinion that the coalition laws need to be reformed (August 1896).

It was then emphatically said that offences against the Prussian law of coalition must be carefully avoided. The closing of the organisation, also, is only rendered possible by the police regarding single committees as associations in the meaning of the law. Thus the announcement of the president of police speaks of an association of 'public confidential agents.' Of such an association people have hitherto known nothing. . . . The committee for choosing meeting places (*Lokalkommission*), which is also designated as an association, consists, if we are not mistaken, of three people. . . . Strange to say, the Central Government of the Social Democratic Party is also regarded as an association. . . . In the legal proceedings, the principal question will probably be, if all these arrangements are to be regarded as associations. The question has a general importance, as, in case of an affirmative answer, all other political parties will be hit. For a Party Government, confidential agents and local associations are possessed by all parties, and that these should have a connection with each other is of the essence of the matter. Also, if the closing of the Social Democratic Associations is confirmed, it will do little harm to Social Democracy. The Party would, at most, transfer its government to a more hospitable state, or to a foreign country. A weakening of Social Democracy is not to be expected from it."

That the dissolution will do no harm to Social Democracy seems certain, for by tradition from the time of the Socialist Law, the central authority immediately becomes vested in the members of the Reichstag—the fraction, as they are called. Now most of the members of the dissolved Party Government, notably the two presidents, the two secretaries, and the treasurer are members of Parliament: these can therefore carry on business as before, and nothing is really changed. The Party chest has been moved to Hamburg, where there is much greater freedom than in Prussia. The Berlin organisation has been restored by a masterly stroke of policy. On December 9, 1895, twelve public meetings were advertised to take place in all parts of Berlin, at which twelve of the leading Socialist M.P.s were to speak. These were not called officially by the Party, but simply advertised " to consider the position to be taken, in view of the dissolution of the Social Democratic Organisation." At the end of the meetings, without a word of warning to any one, a resolution was proposed, protesting against the dissolution, and proposing the election, then and there, of a new confidential agent. At this point, one of these meetings, at which I had the good fortune to be present, was dissolved by the policeman ; the rest succeeded, however, in the election, against which, obviously, the law could have no valid objection. By this step the police were not allowed time to consider, and the essential part of the Berlin Organisation was restored.

II. *Agitation.*—The methods of agitation and propaganda have been admirably described, as they exist in ordinary manufacturing districts, by a Christian Socialist, Paul Göhre, in his book *Drei Monate Fabrikarbeiter.* Göhre was a student of theology who worked for three months as a factory hand at Chemnitz, in Saxony, and thus became intimately acquainted with the life of the ordinary workingman. Although his observations were made just before the expiration of the Exceptional Law, they were made after its administration had become very lax, and are, so far as I could discover by my own observations and inquiries, substantially true of the agitation as it exists to-day. In the following account, almost everything not derivable from official reports, or from my own observations, is taken from this interesting work.

Probably the most effectual of all means of propaganda is the Socialist Press, which is cheap and very widely circulated. There are at present

39	papers appearing daily,	
20	,, ,,	thrice a week,
8	,, ,,	twice a week,
9	,, ,,	once a week,

besides a scientific review, *Die neue Zeit*, and two comic papers, which last have by no means the smallest missionary power. Almost all these papers have a wide circulation; from the official daily organ, *Vorwärts*, which has a circulation of about 48,000, the Party funds derive an annual profit of over 55,000 marks (£2750). Besides newspapers, the Party publishes an immense number of cheap tracts, mostly costing one penny. These contain popular versions of Marx, clear and concise accounts of current questions and current legislation, biting diatribes against Government finance, indirect taxation, military expenditure, &c.—in short, everything best calculated to show that Social Democracy is the working-man's party. Owing to the literary character of the German working-man, these leaflets— often very solid reading—have a much greater effect than an Englishman would naturally expect. People who have come up to Berlin send them, with the Party papers, to their relations in the country, and these hand them round among the rural population. Thus everybody hears of the Socialists as the proletariat party, and when an agitator holds a country meeting, people are interested and go to hear what he has to say.

The next greatest weapon of agitation, after the press, is the public meeting. In Berlin, there is a Socialist meeting almost every night; sometimes two or three. Working-men, often with their wives and families, sit at tables, drinking beer and smoking cheap cigars; the meeting cannot begin till the police arrive, which usually happens about half an hour after the advertised time. Then some one rings a bell, and says " I declare this meeting opened. I request the *Parteigenossen* to choose a bureau" (consisting usually of two presidents and a secretary). Then some one gets up and proposes in a hurried tone three men—or sometimes two men and a woman—who are instantly accepted, and take their places on the platform. These forms are necessitated by the law, and are gone through with the utmost haste. The newly-elected chairman then rapidly calls on the speaker of the evening, who speaks, usually, for a hour or more. He receives little applause, but the closest and most earnest attention. At the end, there is never a vote of thanks, but usually a discussion, in general most orderly and quiet—indeed the whole proceeding is anything rather than revolutionary. The men come to be educated, and an air of conscientious desire for knowledge hangs over the whole meeting. Only occasionally, especially in the speeches of the women, there is a note of bitterness—intense and deep, but never hot-headed, impetuous, or foolish. The police take notes of all that is said; at any mention of the Emperor, or of the pillars of Church and State, they prick up their ears, and write with greater vigour than before. Their report is official, and their interpretation, though often ignorantly absurd —for they are far less educated than the average audience—is alone accepted in a law court. If anything is said which they regard as dangerous, they dissolve the meeting, and the people march out singing a German Marseillaise, with the chorus—

> "Der Bahn, der kühnen, folgen wir,
> Die uns geführt Lassalle."

> (We follow that bold path,
> On which Lassalle has led us.)

As a school for public speaking, and as a club for the more earnest apostles of Socialism, the chief part is played by the electoral associations (*Wahlvereine*), which are coextensive with the Parliamentary constituencies. In Berlin these are now dissolved, but in the rest of Germany they still exist, and have existed throughout the Socialist Law, being, as we saw, specially excepted from some of the provisions of the Coalition Law. They are not allowed, however, to admit women, students or apprentices to their meetings, and they therefore seldom call public meetings themselves. These are usually called by the confidential agent, or some other private member. The electoral associations consist, in flourishing districts, of from 100 to 200 members, and here young members get their training, and debatable questions are discussed. In public, the Party shows, usually, a perfectly united opinion, but in these small meetings the most animated discussions are frequent. Here the opinions of the official party are formed, and here the small minority of *élite* Social Democrats, as Göhre calls them, refresh their faith and determine their local tactics.

But the electoral associations are, after all, little more than a school for those already convinced. The really effectual part of the agitation is carried on by their members, individually, in the course of their daily work, in Sunday walks with their pals, in talks on the way to and from the factory. In personal influence of this kind, Social Democracy derives great strength from the completeness of its gospel; those who are really imbued with its doctrines have a complete philosophy of life, which makes their most casual words, their mere gestures even, an expression of settled convictions. In this way, and by the perpetual handing round of papers and brochures, the *élite* of the Party acquire a dominion over their less intelligent and less definite companions; these are often very vague as to what Social Democracy is, and may even retain a liking for the military or a disbelief in Communism, totally inconsistent with the Party Programme, while yet vaguely convinced that the Socialists alone have the interests of labour at heart, and that the Socialists alone, in some way not clearly understood, but yet held to be genuine, will try to get higher wages for the working-men. All political struggles are class struggles, says Social Democracy, and we are the party of the proletariat class. This catchword is undoubtedly most effective for agitation, and wherever the opposition of capital and labour is obvious and definite, it has succeeded in winning an overwhelming majority of the working classes. In Chemnitz, according to Göhre, he met only three working-men, in the course of his whole stay, who were not Social Democrats. "Everything here," said one of his companions in the factory, "is Social Democratic, even the machines." But as to what constituted Social Democracy, he says, the majority of his companions were very vague. The final aims of the Party, in particular, appear to have been for the most part rather unpopular : so great a change as the abolition of private property was unintelligible to the average working-man. The opposition to militarism, too—which, in the eyes of any unprejudiced observer, must appear one of the best points in the Party Programme—was not shared, if Göhre may be believed, by any but the official members. As, however, the official members alone are clear as to the aims to be pursued, and alone decide the choice of candidates, their views alone are represented in Parliament, and their views, one may suppose, will more and more become those of the rank and file. Just as the constant influence of Marx's knowledge and completeness gradually won over the official party, so, in all probability, the constant influence of the official party will more and more win over the ordinary voter. For this reason, the views of the rank and file, however different from those which find expression in party literature, do not seem to me to have any great political importance.

III. *Tactics.*—But we must now return to the times immediately following the lapse of the Socialist Law. Bismarck's policy, of punishment first and bribes afterwards, had signally failed; the present Emperor resolved on the opposite course. His famous rescripts of the spring of 1890 — in which, after declaring the necessity of factory legislation and the supreme importance of the social question, he urged the calling of an International Conference for the discussion of labour questions — aroused many hopes of a change in the spirit of the Government. The Conference, it is true, produced only the most trivial results—its recommendations could only be of service to the most backward countries—but still the Emperor desired factory legislation, and his dismissal of Bismarck seemed to prove that he was in earnest in his professions of reform.

Under these circumstances, it appeared, for a moment, as if Social Democracy might abandon its attitude of uncompromising opposition, and admit the hope of amelioration by gradual reform. Von Vollmar, one of the ablest of its leaders, who was followed enthusiastically by most of the South German party, made two great speeches to his constituents in Munich,[1] in which he urged the adoption of this policy. Any other attitude, he said, was unworthy of a great party; now that they were stronger than any other single political party, the Socialists could afford to treat with their opponents. The Government had, at last, adopted a conciliatory tone; let them do the same, and hope for an end of the war.

[1] *Eldoradoreden.*

As the terms of a compromise, Vollmar proposed five points :—

(1) Extension of the Factory Laws.

(2) A real right of coalition.

(3) Cessation of all State interference, in favour of one section of society.

(4) Legislation against industrial rings.

(5) Abolition of taxes on the necessaries of life.

But under the Socialist Law, there had arisen in Berlin, the centre of Prussian bureaucracy, a party which, fresh from the oppression of the state of siege, would hear nothing of compromise, of treaties with the Government, or of legal means for gaining the ends of Socialism. Between these two opposing tendencies, the central government of the Party, to avoid the dangers of a split, thought it wisest to adopt a middle course. Bebel, who defined the orthodox position at the Congress of 1891, stated it as the present purpose of their parliamentary activity, not to win this or that concession, but to enlighten the masses as to the position of the other parties, and to make it clear, that these parties denied to labour the most just and elementary demands.[1] But since, as a matter of fact, he continued, parliamentary action *had* this effect, since the winning of the masses was essential to the victory of Social Democracy, they must not hastily adopt revolutionary tactics, but must continue, as before, to agitate for the spread of their views among the working classes, without hoping for concessions from any of the bourgeois parties. In spite of an able defence by Vollmar, Bebel's resolution was adopted, which

[1] *Protokoll* for 1891, p. 174.

declared that no compromise with capitalism was possible, and that no ground existed for changing the traditional tactics of the party;[1] but that forcible revolt was out of the question, and that parliamentary activity was to be pursued with all possible energy as a means of agitation.

Whether this decision was wise or not, it seems impossible for a foreigner to estimate. It is certain, at any rate, that all liberal-minded opponents of Social Democracy regard it as a fatal mistake; but this speaks, perhaps, rather for it than against it. In any case, it is thoroughly consistent with the whole spirit of Marxianism. The utter failure of Lassalle's attempt at negotiation, the brutality of the Socialist Law, and the general intractability of the Government and its supporters, had doubtless persuaded the Socialists that any relaxing of their opposition would only be used to further the ends of the Crown and the aristocracy, and that sheer terror was the only motive which could force the ruling classes into measures of real reform. Bismarck himself had confessed in the Reichstag the justice of this view. "If there were no Social Democracy," he had said during the Socialist Law, "and if many were not afraid of it, even the moderate progress, which we have hitherto made in Social Reform, would not have been brought about."[2] German history certainly lends colour to this view, and the decision of the Party, though in England it would have been madness, may have been a necessary outcome of the boundless selfishness of the German Government. At the same time, its necessity can

[1] *Protokoll*, p. 157.   [2] Speech of November 26, 1884.

only be temporary. The stronger the Party becomes, the more Bismarck's *do ut des* becomes a possible basis of negotiation, and the more peaceful and gradual reforms become feasible without danger of betrayal. We must hope, therefore, in any case, that the Party's *future* policy lies with Vollmar and moderation.

IV. *The Erfurt Programme.*—The same congress which defined the orthodox tactics, the Erfurt Congress of 1891, also defined the orthodox creed, which is still embodied in the Erfurt Programme. The Gotha Programme of 1875, the result of a compromise between the followers of Lassalle and those of Marx, had long ceased to express the general opinions of the Party. As early as 1873, a prominent Social Democrat, W. Bracke, had written a very convincing pamphlet against Lassalle's State-supported productive associations; any but a people's state, he said, would use them as mere means of bribery and instruments of the reaction, while the People's State, when it is once established, will have more thorough means of reform at its disposal. But the demand for these associations remained in the programme, at first because the Lassalleans were still numerous, and afterwards because it was impossible, under the Socialist Law, to undertake so important a task as the revision of the programme. Twelve years of oppression, however, had persuaded a large majority of the Party that they could not accept help from the existing State, and had forced on them the necessity of uncompromising class-warfare. Thus the last remnants of Lassalle's influence had died out, and the Party was ready to adopt a completely Marxian programme.

Accordingly a commission was appointed at Halle to draw up a new programme, and this programme was accepted, in 1891, by the Congress at Erfurt, and has since been the official programme of the party. It runs as follows : —

PROGRAMME OF THE SOCIAL DEMOCRATIC PARTY OF GERMANY.

The economic development of bourgeois society leads necessarily to the disappearance of production on a small scale (*Kleinbetrieb*), the principle of which consists in the worker's owning the means of production. This economic development separates the worker from his means of production, and transforms him into an unpropertied proletarian, while the means of production become the property of a comparatively small number of capitalists and great landlords.

Hand in hand with the monopolising of the means of production, goes the supplanting of scattered small businesses by colossal businesses, the development of the tool into the machine, and a gigantic growth of the productivity of human labour. But all the advantages of this change are monopolised by the capitalists and great landlords. For the proletariat and the sinking intermediate layers—small masters, peasants—it betokens growing increase of the insecurity of their existence, of misery, of oppression, of slavery, of humiliation and of exploitation.

Ever greater grows the number of the proletariat, ever more extensive the army of superfluous workers, ever sharper the contrast between exploiters and exploited, and ever bitterer the class-warfare between bourgeoisie and proletariat, which divides modern society into two hostile camps, and is the common characteristic of all industrial countries.

The chasm between propertied and unpropertied is further widened by crises, rooted in the essence of the capitalistic method of production, which grow ever more far-reaching and more ravaging, which make general insecurity into the normal condition of society, and furnish the proof that the productive powers of modern society have outgrown its control, that private property in the means of production is irreconcilable with the due application and full development of those powers.

Private property in the means of production, which was formerly the means of securing to the producer the possession of his own product, has to-day become the means of expropriating peasants, handicraftsmen and small producers, and of putting the non-workers, capitalists and great landlords in possession of the product of the workers. Only the conversion of capitalistic private property in the means of production—land, quarries, and mines, raw material, tools, machines, means of communication—into common property, and the change of the production of goods into a socialistic production, worked for and through society, can bring it about that production on a large scale, and the ever-growing productiveness of human labour, shall develop, for the hitherto exploited classes, from a source of misery and oppression, into a source of the highest well-being and perfect universal harmony.

This social change betokens the emancipation, not only of the proletariat, but of the whole human race, which is suffering under the present conditions. But it can only be the work of the working classes, because all other classes, in spite of conflicts of interests among themselves, take their stand on the ground of private property in the means of production, and have, for their common aim, the maintenance of the foundations of existing society.

The struggle of the working class against capitalistic exploitation is of necessity a political struggle. The working class cannot carry on its economic contests, and cannot develop its economic organisation, without political rights. It cannot bring about the transference of the means of production into the possession of the community, without having obtained political power.

To give to this fight of the working class a conscious and unified form, and to show it its necessary goal—that is the task of the Social Democratic Party.

The interests of the working classes are the same in all countries with a capitalistic mode of production. With the extension of the world's commerce, and of production for the world-market, the position of the worker in every country grows ever more dependent on the position of the worker in other countries. The liberation of the working class, accordingly, is a work in which the workmen of all civilised countries are equally involved. In recognition of this, the Social Democratic Party of Germany feels and declares itself to be *one* with the class-conscious workmen of all other countries.

The Social Democratic Party of Germany does not fight, accordingly, for new class-privileges and class-rights, but for the abolition of class-rule and of classes themselves, for equal rights and equal duties of all, without distinction of sex or descent. Starting from these views, it combats, within existing society, not only the exploitation and oppression of wage-earners, but every kind of exploitation and oppression, whether directed against a class, a party, a sex, or a race.

Proceeding from these principles, the Social Democratic Party of Germany demands, to begin with:

1. Universal, equal, and direct suffrage, with secret ballot, for all elections, of all citizens of the realm over twenty years of age, without distinction of sex. Proportional representation, and until this is introduced, legal redistribution of electoral districts after every census. Biennial legislative periods. Holding of the elections on

a legal holiday. Compensation for the elected representatives. Abolition of every limitation of political rights, except in the case of legal incapacity.

2. Direct legislation through the people, by means of the rights of proposal and rejection. Self-determination and self-government of the people in realm, state, province and parish. Election of magistrates by the people, with responsibility to the people. Annual voting of taxes.

3. Education of all to bear arms. Militia in the place of the standing army. Decision by the popular representatives on questions of war and peace. Settlement of all international disputes by arbitration.

4. Abolition of all laws which limit or suppress the right of meeting and coalition.

5. Abolition of all laws which place women, whether in a public or a private capacity, at a disadvantage as compared with men.

6. Declaration that religion is a private affair. Abolition of all expenditure of public funds upon ecclesiastical and religious objects. Ecclesiastical and religious bodies are to be regarded as private associations, which regulate their affairs entirely independently.

7. Secularisation of schools. Compulsory attendance at the public national schools. Free education, free supply of educational materials, and free maintenance in the public schools, as well as in the higher educational institutions, for those boys and girls who, on account of their capacities, are considered fit for further education.

8. Free administration of justice, and free legal assistance. Administration of the law through judges elected by the people. Appeal in criminal cases. Compensation of persons unjustly accused, imprisoned, or condemned. Abolition of capital punishment.

9. Free medical attendance, including midwifery, and free supply of medicines. Free burial.

10. Graduated income and property-tax for defraying

all public expenses, so far as these are to be covered by taxation. Duty of self-assessment. Succession duties, graduated according to the amount of the inheritance and the degree of relationship. Abolition of all indirect taxes, customs, and other economic measures, which sacrifice the interests of the community to those of a privileged minority.

For the protection of the working classes, the Social Democratic Party of Germany demands to begin with :

1. An effective national and international legislation for the protection of labour on the following principles :—

(*a*) Fixing of a normal working day, which shall not exceed eight hours.

(*b*) Prohibition of the employment of children under fourteen.

(*c*) Prohibition of night-work, except in those industries which, by their nature, require night-work, from technical reasons, or for the public welfare.

(*d*) An unbroken rest of at least thirty-six hours in every week for every worker.

(*e*) Prohibition of the truck-system.

2. Supervision of all industrial establishments, investigation and regulation of conditions of labour in town and country by a central labour department, district labour bureaus, and chambers of labour.

3. Legal equality of agricultural labourers and domestic servants with industrial workers; abolition of the laws concerning servants.

4. Confirmation of the right of coalition.

5. Taking over by the Imperial Government of the whole system of working people's insurance, though giving the working people a controlling share in the administration.

This programme calls for little comment. The only points of importance about it are its perfectly orthodox Marxianism, and its boundless democracy,

which includes the demand for the equality of men
and women.   As regards the first, it is noticeable
that it in no way distinguishes between agriculture
and other branches of production, and that it sees
no difference between landlord and capitalist farmer.
These two confusions, which it inherits from Marx,
have caused the present difficulties of the Party as
regards the agrarian question, which I shall have
to discuss in the next lecture.   As regards the
second point, the democratic proposals of the programme — referendum, election of magistrates, &c.—
I have neither space nor knowledge for a critical
discussion of them.   But one remark seems necessary, in explanation of their apparently excessive
demands.   Germany has suffered so frightfully from
autocratic officialism, the German official so readily
forgets the interests of the people in the dignity
of his office, and German public opinion is so slow
to take up the offences of powerful magistrates, that
a degree of democracy in the administration of the
Law and the Civil Service, which to us would seem
monstrous and absurd, may well seem desirable to
the German democrats.   It seems at least possible,
under these circumstances, that election of officials
may be a necessary preventive of red-tape and of
the officious exercise of power — particularly in a
collectivist State, where the State official would be
a much more powerful and important personage
than he is at present.

At the same time, a democracy such as the
Erfurt Programme contemplates, a democracy whose
principle is, that the ignorant voter is as good a
judge of current questions as the member who has

specially studied them, would, if consistently carried out, undoubtedly make all wise and expert government impossible. Popular election, with freedom for the elected representative, should be the principle of democratic government. The election of mere delegates destroys all possibility of utilising special skill and knowledge in the governors. It is much to be hoped, therefore, that Social Democracy will, in time, eliminate the fallacious maxim that "one man is as good as another;" a maxim on the basis of which no sound government seems possible.

The Erfurt Programme represents the complete victory of Marx's principles, and for purposes of agitation, its Marxianism no doubt gives it more force than an economically sounder programme could possess. But it seems probable that experience, whether in the agrarian question or in practical politics, will gradually, as the party grows more powerful, and therefore less purely a party of opposition, necessitate the admission of views not to be derived from Marx, and probably in part, positively opposed to Marx. Though it is rash to predict, it seems indubitable that, if the party has a future of power at all, it must purchase power by a practical, if not a theoretical abandonment of some portions of Marx's doctrines. His influence is now almost omnipotent, but this omnipotence must, sooner or later, be conquered by practical necessity, if the Party is not to remain for ever a struggling minority.

LECTURE VI

THE PRESENT POSITION OF SOCIAL DEMOCRACY

I. *Programmes and Strength of the various Parties.*

THE success of Marxian Socialism in Germany is largely to be explained by the political *milieu* in which it has grown up. For the growth of Social Democracy, which has been nearly continuous and of unparalleled rapidity, has been enormously assisted by the mistakes or the cowardice of the other political parties. In the last elections, those of 1893, Socialism obtained, in the first polls, 23.3 per cent. of all the votes given. Since that time its growth has, to judge by by-elections, continued at an undiminished rate. Its strength in the Reichstag, however, has never come up to its voting power : thus it obtained, in 1893, 44 seats, while proportional representation would have given a membership of 96. The *Centrum*, or Catholic Party, obtained, as a matter of fact, 96 members for only 19.1 per cent. of the total vote. The reason for this under-representation lies in the fact that Social Democracy has hitherto flourished almost exclusively in the large towns and industrial centres, which, owing to their rapid growth in population, have at present much fewer members than they are entitled to by their numbers. The present

constituencies were determined by the constitution of 1871, and contained at that time a population of 100,000 each. The average population
of an electoral district at the census of 1890 had,
however, risen to 124,454, and this increase was
almost wholly confined to the towns, the agricultural population, especially in the east, having in
general declined. It follows that agriculture is
over-represented, and industry under-represented
to an enormous extent. Many constituencies have
more than 250,000 inhabitants, some more than
half a million, and these large constituencies are
the strongest centres of Social Democracy. Thus
Berlin, with a population of nearly 2,000,000, has
only six members, of whom five are Social Democrats ; in one of its divisions, represented by Liebknecht, 51,000 Social Democratic votes were given,
while no other party obtained more than 15,000,
and the aggregate adverse vote was under 30,000.
By one of the articles of the constitution, a periodical
redistribution is to be made ; but this article—owing,
I suppose, to the support thus obtained for the Crown
and the loyal aristocracy—has hitherto remained, and
is likely long to remain, a perfectly dead letter.

We will return to this question later, but first
it will be well to take a brief review of the parties, their programmes and geographical distribution.
To an English mind, accustomed to the single
division into Liberal and Conservative, and to the
tactical necessity of supporting one or other of the
great parties, the confusion of German politics is
at first very bewildering. Of the Alsatians, Guelfs,
Poles, Danes, Particularists, and even Antisemites,

I will say nothing; these may be safely overlooked in a general review. But even the great parties are far from few. They are as follows :—

(1) The Deutschkonservative Partei.
(2) The Deutsche Reichspartei.
(3) The Centrumspartei.
(4) The Nationalliberale Partei.
(5) The Freisinnige Vereinigung.
(6) The Freisinnige Volkspartei.
(7) The Süddeutsche Volkspartei or Demokratische Partei.
(8) The Sozialdemokraten.

These are arranged from right to left, and as the differences between some of the contiguous groups are small, we need not consider them all separately. Thus the *Deutschkonservative Partei* and *Deutsche Reichspartei* may be taken together, and so may the *Nationalliberale Partei* and the *Freisinnige Vereinigung*, as also the *Freisinnige Volkspartei* and the *Süddeutsche Volkspartei*. Most of the parties as they at present exist are traditional descendants of parties constituted either in the democratic struggles of 1848 or in the pursuit of German unity. With the exception of the *Centrum*, which is merely Catholic,[1] they are classified by the Social Democrats according to the economic interests they advocate. To Social Democracy, every political party is wholly constituted by economic motives, and without rigidly adhering to this view, it may be well, in considering their

---

[1] Even for this party, Bebel succeeded in inventing an economic motive in his speech on Antisemitism at the Party Congress of 1893 (*Protokoll*, p. 231).

relation to Social Democracy, to adopt this principle of classification.

The Conservative parties, then, represent the interests of the feudal aristocracy : they are essentially an agrarian party, and their chief stronghold is East Prussia, among the large domains of the *Junker*, or landed aristocracy. Their motto is ironically said to be, " Der Konig absolut, so lang er unseren Willen thut." They know that monarchy is their only defence against the democracy, but they have all the turbulence of a feudal oligarchy ; and when agriculture is not sufficiently protected to please them, they can use language for which any Social Democrat would get years of imprisonment. Their programme is pretty much that of George III., a minimum of constitutional government and religious freedom, and a maximum of agricultural protection. They come from the poorest part of the country, and are pecuniarily little better off, as a rule, than our Irish landlords, to whom they have also a great political similarity. The *Deutsche Reichspartei* votes with the Conservatives, but is not so purely aristocratic : it contains some rich merchants and bankers. It always sides with the Government, and, during the reign of Bismarck, was called the party of " Bismarck *sans phrase*." The two parties together obtained at the last election 100 members and 19.2 per cent. of the votes.

The *Centrum* usually holds the balance of power between Liberals and Conservatives, and is thus an important party in Parliamentary tactics. Its vote is in general Conservative, but it opposed Bismarck in the seventies, during the *Kulturkampf* (when its religious freedom was attacked), and on some critical divisions it has opposed extreme measures, *e.g.*, the first introduction of the Socialist Law, and the *Umsturzvorlage* in the spring of 1895. It is generally favourable to the policy of State-Socialism inaugurated by Bismarck, and in spite of its Ultramontanism, it is strictly patriotic. In the elections of 1893 it obtained 96 members and 19.1 per cent of the votes.

The Liberal parties represent the interests of industry and commerce, as opposed to those of agriculture, which are advocated by the Conservatives. The two moderate Liberal parties, the *Nationalliberale Partei* and the *Freisinnige Vereinigung*, represent chiefly industry and manufacture, while the more democratic *Freisinnige Volkspartei* stands, in the eyes of Social Democracy, for banking and the Stock Exchange. The latter view can, however, be hardly maintained; the *Freisinnige Volkspartei* is rather to be viewed as the remnant of doctrinaire *laissez-faire*, favourable at once to free-trade and—in theory at least—to the free right of Coalition, but opposed to State-Socialism. The *Demokratische Partei* is a small but growing South German party, which is more genuinely democratic than any of the other parties. Historically, the National Liberals derive their name and existence from the fight for German unity, but with that reform their energy was spent, and since 1871 they have, at the most, opposed a few retrograde measures proposed by the Government. The *Nationalliberale Partei* and the *Freisinnige Vereinigung* together obtained in 1893,

65 members and about 15 per cent. of the votes, while the *Freisinnige Volkspartei* and the *Süddeutsche Volkspartei* or *Demokratische Partei* got 35 members and about 11 per cent. of the votes.

It is to be observed that all the parties promise to be " ceaselessly active in furthering the welfare of the working-man," but all, except the two extreme Liberal parties, are in favour of the present law of Coalition, and unfavourable to redistribution of seats or to abolition of the Prussian *Dreiklassenwahlsystem*.[1] They are determined to force reforms from above, and to thwart all efforts at self-help on the part of labour.

The following table gives the constitution of the Reichstag, after the last General Election in 1893, as regards the chief parties, and the constitution which would result from proportional representation :—

	Actual Membership.	Membership which would result from Proportional Representation.
Deutsch Konservativen . .	72 } 100	54 } 77
Deutsche Reichspartei . .	28 }	23 }
Centrum	96	76
Nationalliberalen . .	53 } 67	39 } 53
Freisinnige Vereinigung . .	14 }	14 }
Freisinnige Volkspartei . .	24 } 35	34 } 43
Deutsche Volkspartei . . .	11 }	9 }
Sozialdemokraten . . .	44	93

[1] Practically this is true of all but the small South German Democratic Party ; for the *Freisinnige Volkspartei*, in spite of its professions, has never, even where it had the power, made any effort at reform in these directions.

If out of the first eight parties we reckon the first four to the right, the last four to the left, we get an actual majority for the right of **184**, while proportional representation would give a majority of only 6ʋ. This, with the fact that Social Democracy obtained less than half its proper number of members, helps to explain why proportional representation forms part of the official Socialist Programme.

It must be borne in mind, also, that the German constitution is in fact, what the English constitution is in theory, a monarchy which appoints its own ministers, and requires its Parliament for legislation alone. An adverse vote does not cause the Ministry to resign, but only brings about the dissolution of the Reichstag. This leads, of course, to the education of a subservient spirit on the part of members, for a dissolution is always a powerful threat, and where the appeal to the country cannot cause the Ministry to resign, a general election seems as useless as it is irksome. Moreover, the real and pressing danger of war keeps alive the bellicose patriotism engendered by the Franco - Prussian War. This makes a convenient bugbear with which to frighten the country, and an almost certain means of securing the electoral victory to militarism. The Government of Germany is therefore very far indeed from true Democracy, in spite of universal suffrage above the age of twenty-five. It must be confessed, moreover, that the extreme demands of Social Democracy have terrified the nation, and led it to withhold much of the freedom which it might have granted. This terror has had a double effect. While forcing Bismarck and the nation into extensive measures of State-Socialism, *e.g.*, compulsory insurance against sickness and old age, factory acts and nationalisation of railways, it has caused a serious check in the progress of Democracy. The system of property voting by three classes, which prevails in all Prussian elections for municipal and State bodies, would probably have fallen long ago but for Social Democracy. A redistribution of seats, by which industry would have gained an advantage over agriculture, would doubtless also have taken place, and it is not impossible, that the Coalition Laws might have been mitigated by *laissez-faire* Liberalism, whereas now they are being made even more stringent than before. All these possibilities are, of course, merely speculative; but they have had to determine the policy of Social Democracy, and have given rise to the two tendencies, that of moderation and compromise, and that of revolutionary Democracy before all else. It is a questionable wisdom to show one's hand to the extent to which Social Democracy has done so, and it has made its battle a battle for all or nothing, a battle in which no step can be taken until the power is wholly in Socialist hands. Thus nothing can be done until Social Democracy gets the support of the agricultural labourer, and this it has hi\aerto completely failed to accomplish. This brings us to the Agrarian question, and its discussion at the last Annual Congress. How far will Social Democracy be able to solve this question? How far will its programme be found adaptable to agriculture? That is the great question on which its future depends.

II. *The Agrarian Difficulty.*

The discussion of the Agrarian question at the two successive Party Congresses of 1894 and 1895 affords an admirable illustration of the manners of thought prevalent among its members, and contains important indications of future difficulties. I shall therefore deal with it pretty fully.

So long as the towns were, for the most part, still held by hostile parties, there was little purpose in agrarian agitation; the frequent intercourse of towns, the palpable working of economic facts in urban industry, and the great intelligence of the town workers, made these a much more fertile soil for the seeds of Socialism. But when it became obvious that the town workers, except in the Catholic districts, were being rapidly won over, and yet, owing to the shameful preponderance of agricultural representation in Parliament, the number of Socialist members remained comparatively small; when it was seen that anything approaching a parliamentary victory could only be obtained by the help of agriculture, then it became necessary to devote more serious attention to the construction of an agrarian programme. This might seem, to one educated in the opportunist tradition of English politics, no very difficult task; but to the dogmatic German, logic comes before political success, and no programme whose parts contradict each other can be tolerated. Now Germany is chiefly cultivated by peasant proprietors, or by feudal dependents of a feudal lord, who feel an immemorial right to their ancestral holdings. But it is a fundamental prin-

ciple with Marx—a principle accepted in its extremest form by most of his followers—that, in all
branches of production, large businesses tend to
replace small ones. William Whiteley and Huntley
and Palmer are, for Marx, the necessary consummation of all capitalistic industry. Wherever
production on a large scale involves economies, such
a tendency naturally exists, and it is undoubtedly a
merit in Marx to have pointed it out. But it is
absolutely essential, for his theory of economic
development, that this tendency should be unlimited, and should realise itself in all branches of
economic development, for, he says, as the number
of capitalists decreases, the number of the proletariat increases; the latter will still be kept at
starvation wages, while a few capitalists grow continually richer. At last, the proletariat majority
becomes so overwhelming, the contrast of misery
and opulence becomes so glaring, that a revolution
is inevitable. The expropriators are expropriated,
and the proletariat society takes over the means of
production for itself. For it, the wish of Caligula
becomes fulfilled; its enemies come, in time, to
have only a single head, which it can strike off at
one blow. It is obvious that the whole necessity of
the advent of the Socialistic State, as set forth in
this argument, vanishes with the refutation of the
supposed tendency to production on a large scale.
It was impossible, therefore, for the Congress to
declare, with any consistency, that it would support
the peasant proprietor, and avert his impending
ruin. In fact, that ruin was part of the inevitable
process out of which the Socialistic age was to arise,

Every case of bankruptcy on the part of a small cultivator is, for the followers of Marx, so much confirmation of his doctrines; only when the cultivator has sunk into the proletariat, *i.c.*, has been separated from the means of production, and no longer owns his land, only then can he be enlisted in the proletariat army, and begin the fight for collective ownership.[1] This irrefutable logic, strange as it may seem, was accepted at the Congress of 1895 by a large majority of the Party, with what consequences for the agrarian agitation one can as yet only surmise.

Let us now see, more in detail, the process by which this strange decision was reached. There are among Social Democrats, as in all religious bodies, two opposite camps, a Broad Church and an Orthodox Church. The former leans to State-Socialism and compromise; the latter rigidly adheres to the Marxian doctrine that Democracy must be won before all else. The party of State-Socialism is headed by Vollmar, one of the members for Munich; he is an aristocratic Southern German, and has not, like most of the leaders, spent his life almost exclusively in towns and industrial centres. On the contrary, he has devoted much time to the Bavarian peasant, with whose economic condition he is thoroughly familiar. In a speech at the Congress of Erfurt in 1891 he urged a more friendly and conciliatory attitude towards the Government. Bismarck is gone, he said; if we show that wise measures will moderate our opposi-

---

[1] See Bebel's excellent statement of this argument in *Unsere Ziele.*

tion, more will be done for the working-man, and, without abandoning our ultimate demands, we can obtain much to mitigate the present hardships of labour. For this speech he received a severe reproof from Liebknecht and Bebel. " No compromise is possible," said Liebknecht, " between Capitalism and Socialism; and all other parties stand on the basis of Capitalism."[1] " Vollmar would place our ultimate goals and the energetic battle for them," said another leader, Singer, " in the plate cupboard, as a sort of family relic, to be produced only on particularly solemn occasions."[2] The party decided that such a policy was unworthy and time-serving; State-Socialism and compromise were for a time set aside. Again, at the next Party Congress in 1892, Liebknecht emphatically declared, as against Vollmar, that the last fight of Social Democracy would be a fight with State-Socialism. But in 1894, at the Frankfurt Congress, when the question of agrarian policy came up, Vollmar made a masterly speech, setting forth the love of the peasant for his holding, the different nature of town and country, and the untruth, in agriculture, of the tendency to production on a large scale. This tendency, he said, so far as it existed at all, existed only for extensive, not for intensive cultivation; the examples from North American farms, perpetually invoked by Social Democrats, were therefore inapplicable. So far as such a tendency existed in Germany, it was not due to economic motives.[3] We

---

[1] *Protokoll* for 1891, p. 209.   [2] *Ibid.*, p. 198.

[3] It is, in fact, caused mainly by feudal and sentimental motives, and necessitated by the fact that in East Prussia, for example,

must, therefore, he said, promise the peasant something which will make it worth his while to vote for us, and *that* we can never do if we tell him that his plot of ground is to be taken from him by the community. Of the methods hitherto employed in agrarian agitation he gave an amusing and instructive account : [1] " On Sundays, workmen from the town would pour over the country like a swarm of locusts ; they distributed leaflets, often of a very questionable character, and what was worse, old newspapers, full of party squabbles, and often in language not easy for the town workman, but wholly unintelligible to the peasant. Young people, full of zeal for the cause, but ignorant of their task, talked down to the peasants with an air that seemed to say, ' Look here, you blockhead, don't you understand ? ' When the visitors had left the village, you may imagine what the peasants said to one another ! Others, again, went and spoke before the peasants of the materialistic view of history, of the Marxian theory of value, of statistics and other sciences. Afterwards you could read in the Party papers of the great results which had been achieved. But when the fresh laurels of that agitation had begun to wither, exaggerated hopes gave place to mournings and lamentation (*Katzenjammer*)." Vollmar persuaded the Congress that a more sensible method must be adopted in future, and it was decided, by an overwhelming majority, to appoint a commission of agrarian investigation, which should present to

the poverty of the land makes it impossible for any but rich men to hold it.

[1] *Protokoll*, 1894, pp. 144-5.

the next Congress proposals, based on the maintenance of the peasant, so far as the immediate future was concerned, in the ownership of his land. His lot was to be lightened by State action, but Nationalisation was not to be part of the programme.

The Commission, which contained Bebel and Liebknecht and other important members of the Party, sat for a year, and drew up, finally, three proposals, one for North and East Germany, one for Middle, and one for South Germany. These proposals advocated nationalisation of mortgages—the land is mortgaged, *on an average,* to at least one-half of its value, and the mortgages are held by Jews, often the local corn-merchants, who not infrequently get the people completely in their power ; they advocated the maintenance of all sorts of manorial and semi-feudal rights, nationalisation of all ecclesiastical property, abolition of the land-tax, State-schools of agriculture, and in North Germany compulsory associations of peasants, supported by State-credit, as in Lassalle's scheme, for works of drainage, irrigation, &c. Many more proposals of minor importance, but of a similar tendency, were contained in the report of the Agrarian Commission. Their spirit was, on the whole a conservative spirit, since they were intended to prop up a decaying branch of production ; but they seemed eminently suited to please the peasants, and one can hardly doubt that they would have alleviated their extremely miserable condition. At any rate, they were the result of a careful study of the agrarian question, and did not advocate the pessimist *laissez-faire,* which had so naturally failed to win the peasants to the side of reform.

The proposals of the Commission were published some time before the Congress of October 1895, and their publication produced a hot discussion in the press. *Vorwärts*, the official organ of the party, preserved a neutral attitude, but the other Socialist papers became more and more fiery, and for the most part adopted a hostile tone. Thus by the time the Congress came on, people were no longer in an academic frame of mind, and many were very strongly hostile. "We are the party of the unpropertied workmen," said an opponent, who expressed the general view: "we wish to win over the small owner as well, it is true, but only by persuading him that as owner he has no future, that his future is that of the proletariat."[1] Kautsky, the Party theorist, put this view even more plainly: "We must go to the despairing peasant," he said, "and show him that his situation is no transitory one, but arises, by a natural necessity, out of the capitalistic method of production, and that only the transformation of society into the socialistic form can help him."[2] This pessimistic view was based on the Marxian dogma that "everything points to the downfall of small properties, in the country as in the towns."[3] The Party pamphlets, designed to prove this contention, so far as I have been able to get hold of them, confine themselves, as regards agriculture, to rhetoric or vague dogmatism; but the contention itself is, as I remarked before, an essential element in Marxian doctrine, and very

[1] *Protokoll*, 1895, p. 110.   [2] *Ibid.*, p. 125.   [3] *Ibid.*

rigid proofs are, therefore, not demanded by most members of the party. Although Vollmar had ventured on a qualified denial of it in 1894, by denying that Marx has really maintained it, no one ventured, in 1895, to call it in question; we know, said the supporters of the agrarian programme, that the necessary development of capitalistic production cannot be hindered, but we wish to make the transition as painless as possible for the small owners. "I have tested our proposals," said Bebel, "by the following requirements: first, that the capitalistic development of society is not hindered by them; secondly, that they do not contradict the principles of our party; and thirdly, that no burdens are laid on the working classes for the benefit of the owners of land."[1] The Commission were thus forced into an illogical position. While they set forth the practical utility of their scheme they were unanswerable, but when they tried to reconcile it with Marxian doctrines which they dared not deny, nay, which they themselves—with the possible exception of Vollmar—most ardently adhered to, their case was weak, and they were easily demolished by the logicians. "The revolutionising of the masses," said one of the supporters of the Commission, "proceeds not from the head but from the stomach."[2] This, however, was not the view of the majority, and in spite of earnest appeals from Bebel and Liebknecht, the proposals were rejected by 158 to 63. The purely dogmatic nature of this rejection, on the part of most of the opponents at any rate, was well illustrated by a speech on the subject which I heard in a

[1] *Protokoll*, 1895, p. 117.   [2] *Ibid.*, p. 137.

Berlin meeting, by an important member of the Party, in which he said : " We know that small holders of land are doomed to ruin, and cannot, as owners, have any economic future ; for, as our programme tells us, ' the economic development of bourgeois society leads, by a natural necessity, to the destruction of small businesses, whose basis is the workman's private ownership of the means of production.' " This sentence he regarded as sufficient proof of his contention, for which no further evidence was offered.

By the rejection of the agrarian programme the Party have lost for the present, so far as such a prediction can be hazarded, all reasonable hope of winning over the peasant proprietors. The day-labourers, of whom in some parts of Germany there are considerable numbers, might still be won ; they are proletariat within the party meaning of the term ; in the words of the Communist Manifesto, " they have nothing to lose but their chains." These, however, nowhere suffice to win a constituency, particularly as they are, for the most part, fearfully ignorant, and in terror of their employers. Many of them, also, are Catholics, and vote for the Centre, the Catholic party. Owing to the great inequality of agrarian and urban representation, the ruin of agriculture and the growth of the towns cannot give many more seats to Social Democracy, which must, therefore, win over the country if it is to hope for a Parliamentary victory. A forcible revolution would only be adopted in the last resort, as it does not accord at all with the spirit of Social Democracy, which is peaceable and orderly in the extreme. At the same time, Marx's doctrines, derived, as they

were, from the contemplation of English industry in
its days of extreme individualism, are completely
inapplicable to an agriculture carried on either
under feudal lords or by peasant proprietors.
Neither the leaders nor their followers are willing
to abandon Marx, whose theories explain the in-
justice and misery to which they have now to
submit, and promise, at no immeasurably distant
date, a kingdom of heaven on earth, in which
labour shall no longer be exploited, and all human
beings shall be free, equal, and prosperous. This
is the dilemma before which the Party stands, and
on its decision its whole future depends.

Those who have seen the daily support, in the
midst of the most wretched conditions, which the
more intelligent working men and women derive
from their fervent and religious belief in the advent
of the Socialist State, and from their conviction that
historical development is controlled by irresistible
forces, in whose hands men are only puppets, and
by whose action the diminution and final extinction
of the capitalist class is an inevitable decree of fate—
those who have seen the strength, compactness, and
fervour which this religion gives to those who hold
it, will hardly regard its decay as likely to help the
progress of the Party. No, not in a formal and
critical abandonment of any part of Marxian
doctrine lies a tactical solution of their dilemma;
rather it is to be hoped that, like other religious
bodies, like the two chief leaders at the last
Congress, they will lose something in logical acumen,
and adopt, in their political activity, maxims really
inconsistent with their fundamental principles, but

necessitated by practical exigences, and reconciled by some more or less fallacious line of reasoning. The two leaders, so hostile to it in 1891, have now been won over to this attitude of mind, and it is perhaps not too bold to hope that, in time, they may carry the bulk of the Party with them.

There seems, then, at least a *possibility* of peaceful reform and gradual development. *If* the Social Democrats can abandon their uncompromising attitude, without losing their strength; *if* other parties, perceiving this change, adopt a more conciliatory tone; and *if* an emperor or a chancellor should arise, less uncompromisingly hostile to every advance in civilisation or freedom than Bismarck or William II.—if all these fortunate possibilities should concur, then Germany may develop peacefully, like England, into a free and civilised Democracy. But if not, if the Government and the other parties continue their present bigoted persecution, then there seems no power which can stop the growth of Social Democracy, or modify its uncompromising opposition. Sooner or later it is sure to obtain a majority of the whole population, and of a very considerable section of the army. In that case, if it is still repressed, there seem only two possibilities; either an unsuccessful foreign war, by which the military government might be weakened or destroyed; or, if this does not take place, an internal civil war. If Germany could retain its national existence, in spite of such a struggle, we *might* live to see another French Revolution, perhaps even more glorious than the first, leaving Social Democracy to try one of the greatest and

most crucial experiments in political history. But
to all who believe in peace and gradual development, to all who wish the present tense hostility
between rich and poor in Germany to be peacefully
diminished, there can be but one hope; that the
governing classes will, at last, show some small
measure of political insight, of courage, and of
generosity. They have shown none in the past,
and they show little at present; but terror *may*
make them wise, or new men with a better spirit
may grow up. Cessation of persecution, complete
and entire democracy, absolute freedom of coalition,
of speech, and of the press—these alone can save
Germany, and these, we most fervently hope, the
German rulers will grant before it is too late. If
they do not, war and extinction of the national life
are the almost inevitable doom of the German
Empire.

III. *Conclusion.*

Now that our criticism of Social Democracy, point
by point, has come to an end, let us ask ourselves,
lest the final impression should be one of too severe
opposition, what parts of its programme seem essential, and what parts seem chiefly due to the struggling
and persecuted condition of its adherents.

German critics of Social Democracy have, in
general, paid very little attention to the history or
general public opinion of the party, but have confined themselves almost entirely to the programme,
or to chance pictures of the future state. A complete Utopia is, to the German economist, a logically

indispensable part of any Socialistic programme; but however much metaphysics may logically justify this demand in general, every particular Utopia, of course, is more or less of an impossible fairyland, and every particular Utopia, therefore, is triumphantly and gravely shown to be impossible by orthodox economists.[1]

To my mind, however, the really important question is quite a different one. Utopias change from year to year, with the passing fancy of the moment, and in any case the reality is not likely ever to resemble them. The important questions to my mind are these:—

I. What is the essential kernel of the Social Democratic programme, which it could not lose without losing its whole political and historical identity?

II. Are the demands, contained in this inner core of Socialism, in themselves possible or desirable; and are they such as economic and political development is likely to bring about?

The second question involves the whole controversy as to Socialism or Individualism, and as I have no wish to enter on a controversial question, for whose discussion I have not the necessary knowledge, I will only treat of the first of these questions, leaving the second, as to which every reader would, in any case, retain his former opinion, to be decided by each for himself, according to his convictions.

---

[1] Cf. Adolf Wagner, *Die akademische Nationalökonomie und der Socialismus*, 1895; Anton Menger, *Das Recht auf den vollen Arbeitsertrag*, p. 109; Schaeffle, "Impossibility of Social Democracy;" Eugen Richter, *Irrlehren der Sozialdemokratie.*

Even the first question, as to the "quintessence of Socialism," as Schaeffle calls it, is one which cannot, obviously, be answered by a mere study of the programme. To answer it duly, requires, on the contrary, an extensive acquaintance with the ephemeral literature, the speeches, even the daily talk, of Social Democrats, and above all, it requires a sense of the rounded logic of their system, so that mountains and excrescences may not be taken for the regular surface of the world of their ideas. For only by these means can we discover what parts of the programme are believed with most fervour, and what parts could, when events had changed their emotional weight, be altered without serious change of principle or theory.

Under these circumstances, it becomes impossible to prove thoroughly, that this or that item is essential —one must, to an immense extent, rely on mere general impressions. I will, therefore, at once state my own view, and then give what grounds I can to make it seem plausible.

There are, in my opinion, only two items which the Party could not abandon without political suicide, namely:—*Political Democracy* and *Economic Collectivism*—the latter to be brought about by the natural growth of firms, until monopoly becomes the cheapest, and *State*-monopoly the socially most beneficial, form of every business. Around these two essential items, a great undergrowth of minor demands has grown up, especially from carrying the ideals of political democracy into the economic sphere. That these minor demands are now held, in part at least, with great fervour, I should be the last to deny. But they all spring, as I shall endeavour to show, from an excessive passion for Democracy, and are therefore likely, as soon as this passion has been satiated by experience, to fall away of themselves, and leave the essentials to undisputed power.

We in England have all become convinced, by mere brute experience, that Democracy is the only desirable, or at least the only possible, form of Government for a civilised state. But we have also become convinced, and largely by the same brute experience, that the theoretic basis on which the battle for Democracy was fought and won, the extreme individualist doctrine of the Rights of Man, is totally false in theory, and in practice destructive, when logically carried out, of all possibility of social life. In Germany, on the contrary, where Democracy has never existed, political theory is still in the pre-democratic stage: the Conservatives hold a democratic government to be radically bad, or even impossible,[1] while the Socialists advocate it on the old basis of Equality and Natural Rights. It is interesting to observe that the English Socialists of 1820–1840, to whom Marx, and hence the present German party, owe so much, make precisely the same transition, from the extreme Individualism of Natural Right, to Socialism as the only polity in which this ideal can be realised. Thus the Communist Bray says: "Equality of rights is the very soul of society. . . . If a man compel his fellows to give him double allowance of produce for *no labour whatever*, every shadow of equality and justice vanishes

[1] Cf. Schaeffle, *passim.*

at once." [1] It is one of Marx's chief merits that
he eliminated from his theory all trace of this
doctrine, that he developed his communism as the
necessary result of the desires of the proletariat and
the wealth of the capitalists; but his followers, except in controversy with opponents who have misunderstood Marx, usually forget this advance, and lapse
into arguments from Justice and Natural Rights.

A great confusion thus arises, between Marx's
wholly unmoral fatalism, and the purely moral
demand for justice and equality on the part of his
followers. This confusion could not fail to arise,
for Marx's fatalism is based on the moral ideals of
the proletariat and their necessary victory; proletariat disciples of Marx, therefore, as soon as they
work for the realisation of his theories, are forced to
rest their claims on those very moral ideals which
formed Marx's *facts.* Thus it is noticeable that
the first thoroughly Marxian party programme, the
Eisenach Programme of 1869, states, as the first
principle to which members of the Party must
adhere, that "the existing political and social conditions are in the highest degree unjust, and hence
are to be fought with the utmost energy."

I will illustrate this confused reappearance of
the Rights of Man from one of Marx's earliest
popularisers, [2] who, after saying of the Communist
State, [3] "This is no plan which some one sets up,
no purpose to be followed—it is a pitiless *insight*

---

[1] "Labour's Wrongs and Labour's Remedy," 1839, p. 22. Cf. also
Bray's "Three First Principles," p. 28.

[2] W. Bracke, junior, *Der Lassalle'sche Vorschlag.* Braunschweig,
1873. [3] P. 63.

into the nature of things"[1] proceeds:[2] "What is *essential*, is to establish clearly the *principle*, on which the new state of things will be built up. This principle is, socially, a *new conception of property;* politically, the *complete rule of the people.* The *conception of property* in the socialistic society is quite other, but infinitely juster, than that proper to capitalistic production. *To-day* a man earns the more, the more others he can get to work *for him.* The produce of *others'* labour accrues to him, becomes his *own*, makes him rich and independent. *That* is the basis of the capitalistic conception of property: *Property in the labour of others.* In future, every one will have to work for *himself* if he wishes to enjoy. No one who does not work will possess anything, unless indeed he is altogether unfit to work. All property in the produce of *others'* labour will be abolished; for the helpless and for general purposes, however, sacrifices will be willingly made. Property in *one's own* work will be established, and with it, *the holiest, most unimpeachable right of property which can exist.* Nothing belongs to me by right, but the produce of my own work. As, however, production is *in common*, every one must receive his due share of the common produce. To be completely just in this, may have its difficulties. But the socialistic society will always strive to *become* just towards every one. Hence a principle will soon be adopted, which Baboeuf already set up in 1795; the principle: " *To every man according to his needs.*'[1]

---

[1] Italics in the original.   [2] P. 74.

This passage is important, not only as showing the part played by conceptions of justice in current Socialist literature, but also as showing the confusion between reward according to produce, and reward according to needs. Some critics have made very much of the distinction between these two, and have censured German Socialism severely for its supposed advocacy of the latter.[1] The fact is, however, as the above passage and innumerable others clearly prove, that the whole distinction is obliterated, in the minds of Social Democrats, by their principle that all men are equal. For it follows, from this principle, that all would produce equal amounts, and all would require equal amounts. Except for the exceptional cases of invalids, cripples, &c., the distinction would, therefore, be non-existent.

Since Marx is silent on this subject, since Social Democrats themselves are by no means clear about it, and since what they and Marx *are* clear about is the collective ownership of all means of production, it is surely the merest justice to assume, that if ever they were in a position to put collectivism into practice, they would adopt the wisest and most efficient form of collectivism, without dogmatic scruples as to perfect equality of reward. This is the more probable, as Democratic Collectivism, such as they desire, could hardly be put into force except after a considerable period of Democracy, during which period the opposition to practical Democracy would probably cease, and the consequent need to defend it by extreme theories of equality and natural

[1] *Vide* Schaeffle, "Impossibility of Social Democracy," Eng. trans., p. 51.

rights would also cease. Where men or women are hampered, in the pursuit of their most elementary desires, by artificial restrictions and fictitious class inequalities, it seems to them, naturally, the one supremely desirable thing to abolish legal restrictions and recognise the equality of all. Thus we *had* the Rights of Man, and we *have* the Rights of Woman. But as soon as *artificial* inequalities are removed, and a man can no longer acquire superior power but by the consent of others, *natural* inequalities can be recognised without any galling interference with liberty. There is reason to suppose, therefore, if Social Democracy should ever be in a position to carry out its programme, that it will, by that time, have grown beyond its present crude democracy, and be willing to reward the real benefactors of society in any way which may be required by the public good.

Political Democracy and Economic Collectivism, then, are the only demands, if the above discussion be correct, which the Social Democrats are likely to retain if they ever, by a gradual and peaceful development, acquire the supreme power. But if they come into power by a sudden revolution—as they are almost certain to do, unless the ruling classes show a more conciliatory spirit in future—if Social Democrats acquire the government with all their ideals intact, and without a previous and gradual training in affairs, then they may, no doubt, like the Jacobins in France, make all manner of foolish and disastrous experiments. For this reason, again, as for so many others, it is to be hoped, that in future the principle of class-warfare will find less acceptance, and less ground in the conduct of rulers, than it has found hitherto. A wiser attitude on the part of the Government might lead to the victory of Vollmar's less uncompromising policy within the Party, and thus produce a *rapprochement* at both ends. Friendliness to the working classes, or rather common justice and common humanity, on the part of rulers, seem, to me at least, the great and pressing necessity for Germany's welfare. I would wish, in conclusion, to emphasise the immense importance, for the internal peace of the nation, of every spark of generosity and emancipation from class-consciousness in the governing and propertied classes. This, more than anything else, is to me the lesson of German Politics.

LIST OF THE PRINCIPAL WORKS
CONSULTED

ADLER, DR. GEORG. "*Die Grundlagen der Karl Marx'schen Kritik der bestehenden Volkswirthschaft.*" Tübingen, 1887.

ANONYMOUS. "*Nach Zehn Jahren: Material und Glossen zur Geschichte des Sozialistengesetzes.*" 2 vols. London, 1889 and 1890.

ANONYMOUS. "*Das Vereins- und Versammlungsrecht in Deutschland.*" Berlin, Verlag der Expedition des *Vorwärts*, 1892.

ARBEITER - BIBLIOTHEK, BERLINER. *Three Series of Short Pamphlets.* Berlin, Verlag der Expedition des *Vorwärts*, 1891–

BEBEL, AUGUST. "*Die Frau und der Sozialismus.*" 25th edition. Stuttgart, 1895. English translation, "*Woman: Her Position in the Past, Present, and Future.*" London: William Reeves.

BEBEL, AUGUST. "*Unsere Ziele.*" 10th edition. Berlin, 1893. (First edition, 1871.)

BERICHT, STENOGRAPHISCHER, "*Zwei Tage Etatsdebatte.*" Berlin, 1895.

BLISS, W. D. P. "*A Handbook of Socialism.*" London, 1895.

BRACKE, W., Junior. "*Der Lassalle'sche Vorschlag.*" Brunswick, 1873.

BRANDES, G. "*Ferdinand Lassalle: Ein litterarisches Charakterbild.*" 3rd edition. Leipzig, 1894.

BRAUN, DR. ADOLPH. "*Die Parteien des deutschen Reichstages.*"
Stuttgart, 1893.

BRAY. "*Labour's Wrongs and Labour's Remedy.*" Leeds, 1839.

DAWSON, W. H. "*German Socialism and Ferdinand Lassalle.*"
2nd edition. London, 1891.

DAWSON, W. H. "*Bismarck and State-Socialism,*" London,
1891.

ELY, PROFESSOR. "*French and German Socialism.*" London:
Kegan Paul, 1886.

ENGELS, FRIEDRICH. "*Die Entwicklung des Sozialismus von der
Utopie zur Wissenschaft.*" 4th edition. Berlin, 1891.

ENGELS, FRIEDRICH. "*Ludwig Feuerbach und der Ausgang der
klassischen deutschen Philosophie.*" 2nd edition. Stuttgart,
1895.

GÖHRE, PAUL. "*Drei Monate Fabrikarbeiter.*" Leipzig, 1891.
Translated as "*Three Months in a Workshop.*" London:
Sonnenschein, 1895.

HERKNER, DR. HEINRICH. "*Die Arbeiterfrage.*" Berlin, 1894.

"*Hochverraths-Prozess, Der, wider Liebknecht, Bebel, Hepner vor
dem Schwurgericht zu Leipzig vom* 11 *bis* 26 *März* 1872."
Berlin, Verlag der Expedition des *Vorwärts,* 1895.

HODGKIN. "*Labour Defended against the Claims of Capital.*"
London, 1825.

KAUTSKY, KARL, UND BRUNO SCHOENLANK. "*Grundsätze und
Forderungen der Sozialdemokratie.*" Berlin, 1894.

LAFARGUE, PAUL. "*Die Religion des Kapitals.*" London, 1890.

LASSALLE, FERDINAND.. "*Reden und Schriften,*" mit einer bio-
graphischen Einleitung. Edited by Ed. Bernstein. Berlin,
1893.

MARX, KARL. "*Misère de la Philosophie.*" Paris, 1847.

MARX, KARL. "*Das Kapital.*" 3 volumes. Hamburg. Vol. i.,
1867 ; vol. ii., 1885 ; vol. iii., 1894. English translation of
vol. i., London, 1891.

MARX, KARL, UND FRIEDRICH ENGELS. "*Das kommunistische Manifest.*" London, 1848. Authorised English translation, "*Manifesto of the Communist Party.*" London : William Reeves, 1888.

MEHRING, FRANZ. "*Die deutsche Sozialdemokratie. Ihre Geschichte und ihre Lehre.*" 3rd edition. Bremen, 1879.

MEHRING, FRANZ. "*Herrn Eugen Richter's Bilder aus der Gegenwart.*" Nürnberg, 1892.

MENGER, ANTON. "*Das Recht auf den vollen Arbeitsertrag.*" Stuttgart, 1892.

"*Protokolle (Reports) über die Verhanglungen der Parteitage der Sozialdemokratischen Partei Deutschlands.*" Berlin. Verlag der Expedition des "*Vorwärts.*"

Reports of International Workmen's Congresses.

RICHTER, EUGEN. "*Die Irrlehren der Sozialdemokratie.*" 87th thousand. Berlin, 1893.

RODBERTUS - JAGETZOW. "*Soziale Briefe an von Kirchmann.*" Berlin, 1851.

SCHÄFFLE, Dr. A. "*The Quintessence of Socialism.*" English translation edited by Bernard Bosanquet. 5th edition. London, 1894.

SCHÄFFLE, Dr. A. "*Impossibility of Social Democracy.*" Authorised translation. London, 1892.

SOMBART, WERNER. "*Friedrich Engels : Ein Blatt zur Entwicklungsgeschichte des Sozialismus.*" Berlin, 1895.

THOMPSON, WILLIAM. "*Inquiry into the Principles of the Distribution of Wealth.*" London, 1824.

THOMPSON, WILLIAM. "*Appeal of one half of the Human Race, Women, against the Pretensions of the other half, Men, to Retain them in Political, and thence in Civil and Domestic, Slavery.*" London, 1825.

WAGNER, Dr. ADOLPH. "*Die akademische Nationalökonomie und der Socialismus.*" Berlin, 1895.

WOLF, Dr. JULIUS. "*Sozialismus und kapitalistische Gesellschaftsordnung.*" Stuttgart, 1892.

Note.—All Socialistic literature can be obtained from the "Verlag der Expedition des *Vorwärts*," Berlin, S. · W. Beuthstrasse.

INDEX

THE END